Choice

An Autobiographical Journey out of Darkness

Angela Michelle

iUniverse LLC
Bloomington

CHOICE
AN AUTOBIOGRAPHICAL JOURNEY OUT OF DARKNESS

Copyright © 2013 Angela Michelle.

All rights reserved. No part of this book may be used or reproduced by any means, graphic, electronic, or mechanical, including photocopying, recording, taping or by any information storage retrieval system without the written permission of the publisher except in the case of brief quotations embodied in critical articles and reviews.

iUniverse books may be ordered through booksellers or by contacting:

iUniverse
1663 Liberty Drive
Bloomington, IN 47403
www.iuniverse.com
1-800-Authors (1-800-288-4677)

Because of the dynamic nature of the Internet, any web addresses or links contained in this book may have changed since publication and may no longer be valid. The views expressed in this work are solely those of the author and do not necessarily reflect the views of the publisher, and the publisher hereby disclaims any responsibility for them.

Any people depicted in stock imagery provided by Thinkstock are models, and such images are being used for illustrative purposes only. Certain stock imagery © Thinkstock.

ISBN: 978-1-4917-0961-0 (sc)
ISBN: 978-1-4917-0963-4 (hc)
ISBN: 978-1-4917-0962-7 (e)

Printed in the United States of America.

iUniverse rev. date: 9/30/2013

With many thanks to those who helped me
on my journey out of darkness.

Table of Contents

Introduction

I sat on the subway surrounded by the afternoon commuters, so many people crammed into such a small place, everyone focused on their own agendas and thoughts. I started wondering about the faces I saw, curious about the stories they have. My eyes turned to look at a penny by my foot and I started thinking about my own stories. The last remaining gift from my father was a penny.

After arriving home, I went to the small pill container in my jewellery box that kept my memories safe. The circular tin looked hardly aged, even with decades passed. I slowly opened the container, unsure as to all the items I'd put in over the years and the memories contained within; each one a chapter in my life.

I had kept so many journals over the years. I spread them out on my bed. My writings sucked me into a time warp, to the moment in time that I wrote my thoughts, feelings and experiences. Now with the items once again in my hand and journals before me, everything returned with intense clarity.

Childhood images flashed before my eyes. I grew up in a small town and experienced more than my share of trauma. I was the second youngest of four children in a home that often had police come by and children's aid involved. My family was a mess, but it was that trauma that pushed me in the opposite direction, urging me to escape and find normalcy. I made it through high school and left home for university determined to forge my own path.

I believe I made it. Now married with two children, I have years of therapy behind me. The façade of normalcy I strived to maintain is no longer necessary. Everything that seemed so intense before has simply turned into a story. Often I talk with others who have experienced trauma and discuss the feeling of isolation that accompanies such experiences. There are many paths to healing, for some time will heal wounds, others need to tell their story, and others need to be there for others experiencing trauma. My healing required all three paths.

My Early Years 1980–1990

The elusive innocence of childhood

1

Hidden Secrets

The container was almost as significant as the contents. I saw it and thought of the prescriptions that built my façade. I remembered choosing one that depicted two young girls with their arms around each other. It reminded me of my sister Emily. She is two years younger than me and was often the only thing that kept me going. The earliest memories I had were of Emily, I hid her in the closet under the mountain of laundry to protect her from the violence; on the really bad days we both hid there. There were many memories from early childhood which I'm glad were never recorded in one of my journal entries. They remain only as visual flashes, fading further as time passes.

My dad was a big source of my angst. He parented through fear and punishment. Such fear led to denial of doing wrong in hopes that someone else could take the blame; unfortunately, he belted all of us when we denied our mistakes. He had a quick temper; perhaps that was due to his upbringing, stress or just personality. He loved to hunt, and his gun collection scared me. One fall, he was angry about something when he brought home a deer and said "Watch out, or Rudolph is next."

At Easter after he had bagged a rabbit he said: "Next time it will be the Easter Bunny."

From early on I learned to hate holidays and fear him. I remember just seeing my dad's face or hearing his voice and being afraid. The memory of the last fight is etched in my brain. One of my earliest journal entries described it as: *He was in the basement on a rampage, thankfully not focused on me. I was at the top of the stairs. I heard the kicks, the cries, and the disharmonic echoes of the piano being hit, glad it wasn't me trying to escape his wrath. My mom yelled down to him: "I'm sick of your violence. Come hit me, I'll put a hot pack on it* (to increase the bruising) *and you'll never see these kids again."*

The big presents often came after the big bursts of violence. By the age of six, I had learned when I had leverage to get what I wanted. One day in a motorcycle shop, I straddled a Yamaha Y-Zinger. Everyone said I looked so cute on it so I refused to get off. He bought it for me. I remember practicing on it most of the morning then getting my mom to come out and watch me. I turned back to see her reaction and crashed into the telephone pole. Emily, also a novice, drove around the outhouse stuck in a wheelie that wouldn't release until my brother Billy intervened. Shortly after that the helmet got a name tag reflective of Evil Knievel. We'd zip that bike around our block and out at the cottage. We were the envy of all the four-to eight-year-olds.

Billy was biking with me the day I had my big wipe out. I was driving down a steep hill on a dirt road out at the cottage. I almost did a complete flip – my feet went over the handlebars, then the bike landed on top of me and I was face down in the gravel road. I was in tears. Billy commented on what an amazing flip that was. I refused to get back on the bike and he managed to convince me that we needed to go and tell everyone what a great stunt I just did. We were back to the cottage within ten minutes. Emily and I got hooked on bikes, then moved up to the bikes my brother outgrew, a Harley Davidson 90, also known as our "Hardly Davidson" then a Yamaha 175.

Our neighbourhood was an interesting mix of individuals. Some neighbours always knew what was going on but remained quiet. Some neighbours were protective and acted to help us, like the ones who called my mom when someone was trying to get me to light her cigarette when I was in grade one, putting it in my mouth and telling me to breathe in. Some neighbours were abusive and violent, like the ones who killed our cat. The pictures they left in our mail box with our cat's charred body showed them as they burned our cat, swung him by his tail and buried him alive.

When we started family therapy, the therapist told me "You need to stand up for yourself."

She told everyone else to leave the room. When I still refused, she left the room for a moment and then came back and told me "I've sent them all home."

"My mom would never leave me." I told her.

She showed me that the waiting room was empty. I was alone. "You need to scream." she told me.

I started crying. I sat there abandoned by my whole family, totally alone, with a supposed trusted therapist. After a while, she drove me home, stopping to buy me ice cream along the way. I wonder now if she felt guilty for using such an unethical form of behaviour modification.

After the separation it took time before we started to visit dad. We had the protection of Billy until Billy finally stood up to him. The first night Emily and I stayed at Dad's alone, I couldn't handle it. In tears of fear, scared to be alone with him, I called our mom, and she picked us up and took us home. Being anywhere without the protection of my brother or mom was hard.

There was a holiday party when I was taken to a bedroom, and the guy took down his pants and tried to make me to do things to him. His sister made a noise in the closet, and when he turned to see the noise, I ran away. I tried to tell but no one there believed me and he said I was lying. I called my mom. Why would I make it up? At least she came to pick us up and we left.

Once when I was ten, I was at my best friend Tanya's house, playing with her younger sister Dawn in the camper they had in their driveway. Her mom told us we needed to come inside; my mom had called. My mom showed up with Emily and our pyjamas; we were going to spend the night and had to stay inside until the police were done. We watched the movie *Space Camp* and I cried telling her that my life was such a mess. I'm so thankful for having a good friend like Tanya. Her family moved a lot and we became pen pals when they weren't in town. We kept writing throughout elementary school and most of high school. Sometimes the letters slowed down, but even with the transition to university there were still a few sporadic letters. She remained a constant in my life and was the only person at my wedding from my early years.

Still, as much as that container holds hidden secrets, it is just a hard metal vessel that has served its purpose over the years. It holds so many flashes of early childhood memories. I am forced to remember my natural instinct to survive and all the universal strength that I've felt come to me when I've lost my own.

It was in *grade seven, March 22nd 1989, that I felt I had the power of She-Ra, "the most powerful woman in the universe." within me and at my disposal. I don't remember what happened to start it all, but everything* got intense fast. She was a known abuser, and had me pinned against the couch. One hand was choking me, the other delivering intense blows. I couldn't breathe and I thought this time I was actually going to be killed. I struggled without success. There was nothing I could do physically; I needed help. Searching for something, anything, my gaze landed on the coffee table. There were dishes, and luckily for me, a steak knife. I grabbed it with the last of my remaining strength and brought it straight to her neck, the serrated edges of the blade indenting her skin, forcing her to back off a bit as I snatched a breath of air. I yelled "get off of me!"

I moved as she moved, the knife still on her throat, yet she still wouldn't let go of me. It was almost as if she was daring me. "If you ever touch me again I will cut you right open." All the hatred was pouring out of me. I felt ready to kill her right then and there. It would be self-defence, I reasoned; I'd be cleared, so there was nothing holding me back! But that voice inside me said my life would change with her blood on my hands. I couldn't do it. I needed to get out of the house. I held the knife in my hand, pointed at her, as I backed up to the door. I grabbed my bag and ran to school. The office was open; I broke down in tears as I told them what happened. They called my mom to inform her about the incident and the abuser was taken away.

2

Happy Memories

I glanced away from the container itself and started to focus on the variety of token keepsakes before me. The smiley face was just a circle of paper out of a hole punch that Cory drew on then gave to me during class. Cory always brought a sense of joy to any situation. He was one of those guys that Emily and I had fun with. He was cute, smart, silly and could seemingly easily switch from light-hearted play to serious discussions, both of which I needed. Cory's method to return to a serious mindset from a silly one was amusing: "Just think of dead puppies." he said, "it can stop you from laughing at any inappropriate moment." It became a regular phrase between us. As much as the smiley face reminds me of Cory, it reminds me that he challenged me to find good memories. Some happy memories were easy to bring to mind, while others took years of therapy and soul searching to find peace within the memory.

My favourite childhood happy memory is Halloween! It is the only holiday without extended family, and often just Emily and I running through the streets with friends. My mom always made us amazing costumes; Emily and I would keep them and cycle through different ones every year, doing multiple trips around the neighbourhood. We would drop off our bags at home so Mom could hand out the stuff we didn't like. Our candy often lasted us until summer. Every year, Mom would take our suckers and melt them down for Christmas baking or stain glass creations. Her baking was the best part about Christmas.

My favourite Christmas was the year Mom took us to a friend's place. It was the perfect day for a walk amongst all the snow-covered trees. We wore snow shoes and walked peacefully through the woods. I remember looking up at the blue sky from beneath the umbrella of trees thinking this is what Christmas should be. I don't remember if we were choosing a tree for us or them, but returning back to their house and having hot chocolate established this adventure as the epitome of Christmas to me.

The one thing my dad did that I truly loved was fishing. I love water. Whether or not I had a rod in my hand, I loved being on the boat, with the warm sun shining down. My mom took us to the marina all the time, perhaps another reason I love water. It always brought a sense comfort and peace. Whether we were feeding the seagulls, stopping for a burger or just sitting and watching the boats, water was my solace. The marina was a safe place that always brought happy memories.

One of my first best friends was Scott. We were in kindergarten together; he lived only three houses away from us on the other side of the street. He was my escape for two years. We would always play in the small forest behind his house. It seemed that whenever my world was messed up or falling apart, he was there. He moved away in grade one and I never saw him again. I'm not sure if one can fall in love in kindergarten, but he was the first to capture my heart. From the simple "I'll show you mine if you show me yours" young exploration, to the dependability and consistency that came from knowing he would always be there.

I remember Scott every time I have tomato soup. His mom regularly made it for our lunch after kindergarten. I think it was the only time I had tomato soup, but the memories of peace and friendship have always remained strong. I've tried to search him out a few times, but never found him.

Tracy was another great escape. We went to school together from kindergarten to grade eight. She was a tom boy like me, and we organized baseball and basketball games and spent afternoons and weekends just hanging out with the guys playing sports. I have lots of great memories of us playing on those fields behind the school. Many of them were before puberty and never made it into a journal.

Emily played an integral role in my good childhood memories. We rode our bikes, played at the park, and developed interesting schemes and messed with people's minds. As cruel as it may appear, I think it was mostly to get attention from boys we liked. Colin was a significant receiver of our plans. He was a boy in my class since kindergarten. For three years, I made the Valentine's box for our class and always gave him the biggest valentine I could find in the store that would fit in the box, signed 'your secret admirer.' It drove him crazy. He asked everyone, even the principal, if they had given it to him. February 12th, 1988: *Someone told Colin I sent the card. He doesn't seem too upset though.*

Emily and I would also play with our voices and call Colin, set up a fake date at the skating rink and then go and hang out with him, chatting or skating with him while he waited for someone who never showed. In reflection he must have meant a lot to me, as we seemed to put a lot of effort into spending time with him.

June 24th, 1988 had an all encompassing entry about a party, my mom and my first recorded dream. *Jason was having an end of year party; we were finishing grade six. He always had big parties and invited most of the class. Many of us were together since kindergarten. It was fun. I went swimming, played a game of pool with Colin and then went in the hot tub. Jason's house is so cool. He always had alcohol at his parties and we'd play games like truth or dare and spin the bottle. When Mom picked me up it was 11:30 and she took me to McDonalds. We ordered and it took forever to get our food. After the first five minutes, she turned the car off and when the lady brought us our food my mom told her she's going to have to call a tow truck because we ran out of gas while we were waiting. The lady looked at us and the line up behind us; then ran away in a frazzled state. Mom then turned the car back on and drove off.* It was a critical party for so many reasons. I watched *Nightmare on Elm Street,* which left a lasting impression. It also reminded me of the things my mom did for me; driving to and from parties, getting us late night snacks and surprising me with her unpredictable humour.

It was after that party, and that movie, that my dreams became paranormal. I was 12 years old and Freddy Krueger became real to me. I started waking up from horrible nightmares, reliving a moment from the movie in which I was fighting Freddy. The places he injured me in the dream would often have minor scratches or bruising. I tried to convince myself that it was some strange coincidence, but the nightmares and injuries continued. I will never forget the worst of the dreams.

He got me again. I ran to Emily's room and crawled into bed with her. I can't sleep, I'm too scared to close my eyes. It was so windy that the noise was keeping me up. I tried singing songs in my head to relax, but Freddy kept coming back, entering my sleepy thoughts: "One, Two, Freddy's coming for you…"

Every time I'd dismiss him, he would only return again. Suddenly I was a character in the movie. I had images of watching TV, just like that character who burned themselves with a cigarette to stay awake. I must have drifted asleep, because I felt I was in the movie, but I knew it wasn't me. I knew it was a dream, but he was there, in my room, under my bed.

I woke up. "It was just a dream." I told myself. But the song was still in my head.

Then I heard him and the cutting sounds coming from the bottom of my bed, through the mattress. I jumped up. He easily cut through my bed and said "Now you're mine!" He was staring into my eyes, and grabbed my arm.

As I ripped it away he sliced my arm open. I felt every sensation as he cut me, the pain and the blood pouring out. Looking at the blood, I screamed. The scream was so loud I woke myself up. This time I needed to prove I was really awake. I needed the lights on. I jumped out of bed landing far enough to be out of an arm's reach from anyone or anything hiding under my bed, and ran to the bathroom. I was so scared. My arm really hurt. I told myself it was just the fresh memory of the dream, but when I went to rub it, my arm really was hurt. There was a long scratch on my arm right where he got me.

In September 1988 I moved up from Navy League and joined Sea Cadets. I learned to use a rifle, tie knots and sail. I learned to follow orders and give them. I wrote my exams and worked my way up the levels. It didn't stop the scary dreams, but there was some power and control I got from giving orders and holding a gun.

On April 3rd, 1989, Tracy was over at my place. We phoned Neil, a boy I'd been in love with since grade four when he transferred to our school. Another classmate answered, *we talked for a bit.*

"Do you want to go to the movies with Neil on Friday?" he asked

"Only if he promises to go." I said.

"I can't promise, but I will try." he said.

We heard them talking in the background. I heard "Angela, Kelty and Crystal."

I asked Neil, "Angela, Kelty and Crystal what?"

"Are the top three girls in the class." he told me. I was all smiles, not expecting the best compliment ever! Of course it was followed only three days later with one of the worst insults ever. *At recess some of Neil's friends were walking past and said "Angela wouldn't be overweight if she was married to a hippopotamus or an elephant."*

Well, it's Friday. He told me he had to cancel the movies. He said it was a family thing and had nothing to do with me…I'm not sure about why he needed to say that. Did that mean it was about me?

I was hanging out with Tracy May 13th and we went for a walk to the creek and met up with Colin and his best friend Graham. They were running by the side of the water and fell in. They were shivering! We kept telling them they'd get warmer faster if they took off their shirts, but they chose to freeze. Maybe that stemmed back to the time my father had found them dancing topless on the freezer, which quickly ended my birthday party in grade one. This group of four was one of my favourites, all of us together from kindergarten. I felt known, safe and free. It was a group of four I trusted. It's interesting to reflect on small moments that never made it into journals but left such a lasting impression. Many adventures with Tracy distracted me from what was going on at home. She and Tanya are the only female friends that lived up to the role of best friend.

October 23rd I was playing basketball with Neil and some of our friends. It started out fun, but it slowed down so I was about to leave. Neil was sitting on my jacket.

"Can you get up so I can have my jacket?" I asked.

"No." he said "you can't have it and you can't leave." Then he got up, took my jacket and ran. I ran after, chasing him. I think he just wanted me to chase him and I just wanted to be alone with him. I finally got my coat, but it was the look in his eyes that convinced me to go back to the basketball court and not home.

The dance was October 31ˢᵗ. Neil and I danced three songs together, two slow songs and one snowball, (one of those dances where they call 'snowball' and you have to quickly find another partner before all the good ones are taken). My favourite one was that one by Berlin, Take My Breath Away, from the movie Top Gun. Neil's arms were together behind me, my arms on his shoulders and his head leaning on my head. We were so close I could feel his heart beating. When it was over, he thanked me. I love him. I wished it would go on forever, but when it stopped it gave meaning to my life and made me believe happiness is obtainable!

December 21ˢᵗ was the best dance ever! It was awesome! Neil and I danced. We were so close. We danced to Bette Midler's The Wind Beneath My Wings and Bad English's When I See You Smile. After our second dance, he held me in his arms a moment longer and then kissed me! It was about one inch below my eye on my right cheek. I love him.

Neil was a pretty strong part of my elementary days. It's almost funny looking back at a young crush and how such small interactions made such a difference. I don't think the highs and lows are ever as intense as when you are a teenager.

3

How the Dreams Began

*W*ow. The sequin dream feels like it was so long ago. This is the token memory that reinforced my dreams have meaning, and my communication with God was validated as being genuine. My mom was always great at listening to my dreams and trying to interpret them. She taught me that dreams can have meanings and messages. She often thought I was making up the dreams because they were so vivid and went on and on and on, but the process of talking about them and reliving them triggered something in my brain that helped me fully remember my dreams.

I often dreamt about war times of long ago, long walks through vast fields with large boulders. There was always the same man at my side; we were hiding out and fighting. All of these dreams happened annually, in June, within a few weeks of each other until one day I saw the guy in my waking life. It was June 17ᵗʰ, 1989. *He knew it was me! Is that even possible? I was at the mall with Kelty when our eyes met. We veered towards each other and stopped.*

"It's you." he said.

"It's you." I replied.

Stuck in a moment, unexplainable, trapped between two worlds, memories of our past life flooded me. I'm not sure how long we were there; it must have been only two minutes, but the memories, images, his words, the connection… I seemed to be sucked into a trance, just long enough for my classmate to ask who that was and what was going on. She pulled my arm and I came back into the moment. The validation of the dream and the connections above and beyond this life made me wonder.

Perhaps that was just the preparation I needed to accept the next dream. It was November 18ᵗʰ, 1989 and one of the most intense paranormal weekends of my life. Emily and I were spending the weekend at my dad's. *I'm freaking out! I'm trying to breathe. It is so messed up! I had a nightmare about my father sexually assaulting me. It was detailed, graphic, real and horribly nasty. God, why would I dream such horror? Is there a chance it happened? Have I simply repressed the memories? I wouldn't be the first to say he had molested them. Is it true? I have to know.*

Then almost as if God was talking back, I heard. "It's true. He'll ask; Are you going to have an omelette for breakfast?" If my dad asks me that, it is full validation. My dad made scrambled eggs but never made omelettes. If my dad asked that question I'd know the dream had meaning.

He asked!!! We went out for breakfast and right there at the stop sign. He turned around in the driver's seat looked at me in the eyes and asked. "So, are you going to have an omelette for breakfast?" My heart stopped. My head started screaming. "No!" *I was shaky, I wanted to open the door, jump out of the car and run away.* "No, I don't know what I want yet." *It's true? Was he in my bed that night? Exhausted, scared, confused and unable to focus, I ordered waffles, but hardly touched them. I was trembling and couldn't find peace. The reason I hated dresses suddenly seemed obvious. I can't go out there. I feel violated. I'm sitting in my room questioning the messages I was receiving through dreams. God is there any evidence that my dreams have meaning? My eyes are glazing, thoughts swirling...I need to turn to logic! So glad I brought my math homework.*

With so much going on, I talked to God extensively in my head before going to sleep. *I had this great dream of semi-formal, with great music and friends. It was the best night ever, so much better than the dances with Neil. I was in a beautiful red sequined dress. I had an amazing time. I woke after the dream, in the middle of the night with my eyes slowly focusing on something lying on my pillow. It was a red sequin from my dress. Somehow that discussion with God, asking for proof, it happened. That sequin appeared. It manifested, from nothing and everything.*

What is happening? *I'm 13! My relationship with God changed. The search for the unknown began, my life somehow a crazy paranormal existence. Purpose? Validity? Meaning? Interpretation? Where do I go? What do I do? Why am I here?*

Grandma is still in the hospital. I hate cancer. She has been getting progressively worse. I had a weird dream last night that felt so random and yet so powerful. I had a dream about a tooth falling out; it was my front top right tooth. It fell out. There was no blood, no pain, it just fell out. I woke up with incredible sadness; I think she is going to die. I don't know if there's a relationship between the dream and the knowing sadness, but I feel she won't be with us much longer.

We had to go to Dad's again this weekend so mom can spend some time at the hospital. I'm still freaking out about the omelette and sequin. He bought us a camera. The big gifts always came after craziness. Did he know about my dream? Was he in my bed that night? Did I sleep through something? I hate being here. I hate the way he looks at me. I can't make eye contact. Mom called and Billy is going to pick us up so we can visit Grandma. Things are getting worse. Emily was thrilled about the new camera and she brought it with us to show our mom. At the hospital, Emily showed the camera to everyone and commented, "We don't have many pictures of Grandma."

Mom responded quickly "Now is not the time to be taking pictures." I took the camera and put it in my coat pocket and we went upstairs to see Grandma. She was in a coma. We all took our turns saying hi. I was standing at the foot of the bed when she sat up completely lucid and looked at me.

"You have the camera." She raised her arm, her finger extended, pointing at me, her eyes penetrating my soul.

"I do." I said meekly, frozen in place.

"Don't take any pictures!" She ordered me. She lay back down, seemingly right back into the coma.

I looked at my mom, sisters and brother, all of us baffled. "Did she just do that?" I asked.

"She was listening." my mom said quietly. My grandmother's spirit had begun travelling outside of her body. Her time on earth is almost over.

It was around this time I turned my back on Christianity. I couldn't continue. Religion just didn't make sense any more. I was baptized Anglican, but Jesus seemed too easy of a path, the "remission of sins" was an easy escape route for any abuser. I had issues with the idea that with just a few prayers and apologies all could be forgiven. How can that work with an abuser? *I often refused to go to church. Mom's so upset now because I refused to go to church again. I can't. I hate being preached to and don't agree with most of what he says. At least she let me stay home. Religion just isn't for me. I need to know people are expected to live spiritually and be good, patient and help others.*

I explored spirituality, God and the experiences I've had, almost as if I was asking to be normal. I learned that the First Nations beliefs were accepting of visions, voices and spiritual guides. Buddhists were accepting of past lives, Karma, enlightenment and energy. Judaism allowed for one God and had biblical references to prophets, divine messaging and intense simplification of science through stories that should not have been understood at the time they were written. All religions have valuable teachings and flaws, but these three systems had something that called to me. Perhaps I was looking for a way to frame my spiritual experiences within the norms of a society.

It was just before 4:30am on November 28ᵗʰ when I woke up. I knew she was gone. I got up to find Mom sitting at the dining table.

"You're up?" she asked.

"I think something is going on with Grandma." I responded.

"Yeah, I woke up to her calling my name." she said, confirming my thoughts.

Moments later Emily joined us. "What's going on?" she asked. Emily sat down as the phone rang. It was the night nurse from the hospital, someone my mom knew.

"Grandma died." my mom said, relaying the message from her co-worker.

Moments like this are starting to seem too normal. Knowing and having a moment to prepare before information presents itself… It is strange to reflect on the clarity I seemed to have before understanding anything contained within. This was a critical period in my life. My dreams started giving me insight and preparatory warning dreams. I started both questioning and trusting, and delving into spirituality in a way beyond most thirteen-year-olds.

So, as if the holiday season wasn't enough, a boy I've been crushing on tried killing himself and another boy in my class was diagnosed with cancer. I knew I wasn't the only one with an intense life and challenges, but it's different when things come up for people I don't expect. Maybe my own slump is making it even worse; so much is going on right now. *Everything is different. The fragility of life, the importance of choices, and the presence greater powers are all converging front and centre for me. There is just too much crazy right now.*

Life

My tear drops are falling for you today,
Whenever I see you I can't look away,
I don't know what I could possibly say,
Except for the words I love you.
I'm sorry you had to go through such pain,
I'm sorry there is no one you can blame,
I know how you feel, wanting for rain,
To hide all your tears so blue.
I just wanted to tell you that I'm here,
Whenever you need a friendly ear,
So you can release your angers or fear,
For you; I will always, always be here.
Angela, 1990

I distracted myself; I put my energy into music, especially my flute and my talent show performance. I got the hat-trick award for consecutive achievements in the talent show and I was the recipient of an award for being a well-rounded, high-achieving student. It came with a cheque for $75 and a ceremonial dinner to present the plaque.

High School 1990-1995

Loneliness grows on the desolate street
in the darkness of the early morning

4

Negotiating Teenage Friendships

I don't know why I chose this small metal ring to represent our friendship. Delia found it on the floor while I was at her place; she gave it to me and I told her "I'll treasure it always." It was early December 1990. I'm sure at that moment she didn't expect me to be holding it in my hand over 20 years later contemplating our friendship. Delia and I met in grade nine; everyone thought we'd been friends longer. We both leaned on each other for support. We'd go for walks together and talk for hours on the phone. We helped each other create some very weird but wickedly fun parties. Everyone always thought of her as the weird one, but she really brought out the crazy side in me. There are a few memories of her that easily come to mind. With her, things were childlike and fun. We would do silly things like stand at one of the more popular corners and wave at people driving by as if we knew them, simply to watch their reactions as they tried to figure out who we were. We also did one of those pointing up to the sky episodes to see how many people we could get to look up to see what we were pointing at. There was nothing there. We were in a small town and there was never anything in the sky. Every time we succeeded, we would start laughing uncontrollably at the person squinting to see what we saw.

Delia and I wrote lots of notes to each other, and kept them in what we called our "green book." It was an interesting read going through those notes, reading them I was instantly transported to the past.

> *It's funny, you know, that people just assume I'm weird because of the way I dress and people assume you are normal because of the way you dress, when, actually, you are just as weird as me and even stranger at times. So there! Know what? I think, next week (for the days I will be here, anyways) you should dress like me and I should dress like you and we could tell everyone that we switched bodies because of some freak accident. Wanna? Wanna?! Ya! Let's do that! Tomorrow. (The day you read this, it will be today.) I'm going to try to attract the least amount of attention to myself. How's that? I'm just gonna sit and not talk and be good and silent and stuff. Then Mr. Dubik will say, "My, what a well behaved child you are" and everyone will say "Where's Dee today?" and I will quietly say "Here" and they will wonder*

what's come over me and I will say "I am going to be like everyone else for one day" and then I will go and buy Club Monaco and Guess Jeans and burn my toque. And then I will cry. Cry and cry and cry. (And cry.) Well, maybe not the last part. I mean, I won't burn my toque or buy those things, or cry. But I will draw a picture of Mr. Cotton in 20 years. Pretty good huh? Actually I traced it from this book called Unlucky Wally. This is really unlucky Wally, Mr. Cotton's twin. I am tired of writing and so I will go to my room and do homework!!! Yours for a long time or longer.

Dee.

Another entry was from around the same time. *I can't believe my father is so dense. Sometimes I just hate him. Here he is blabbing on about the government spending three million on computers. How could they? We are in a recession and the government is spending three million on computers. I feel as though I was born in the wrong time. There are things I want to do and stop but I don't know how. The rainforests are being destroyed, pollution is taking over the world and the government spends three million on computers? Why don't they buy the rainforests back? Why don't they purchase better filters for the factories? I don't know why I was born in this time or town, but if I could start over it wouldn't be in this town. I wouldn't have a father who abused me as a child, or place myself in a spot with so much exposure to abuse.*

If I could start over I would be brought up in a smaller town, live in a house with a large garden, have a father who cares about me and something more than stupid electronics like stereos, computers and TVs. I would live in a town where my words would mean more, so I could do more. I wouldn't pick a time when there was war and unhappiness, suffering and starvation. I would pick a time and place where females were equal, where males understood and where humans could live in harmony with nature.

I'd want to be in a place where there wouldn't be killers, rapists, molesters, thieves or kidnappers. I want to be in a place where all this was possible. I wonder if I will ever get to this place of mine. Maybe not now but Mars is getting an atmosphere and there must be other places in the galaxy and the rest of space. Maybe I could become an astronaut and go to these places. Sometimes I just feel like giving up. I don't really know what to do; I think about killing myself. God will just put me back in the same situation I'm in now or worse, maybe. There is a lesson I'm supposed to learn here. I don't know what I did in my last lifetime to deserve this. Maybe I was a mass murderer or a child molester. But I'm still getting it back worse than I could ever have given it. I would've had to have killed or molested over 1000 people and destroyed all of their families to deserve what I'm getting now. Maybe I was the one who gave fathers the idea to molest their children.

I don't know. Maybe I don't deserve to live. Maybe I deserve worse that what I am getting. Maybe I'll marry an axe murderer to help straighten me out. Sometimes I wonder why God gave me brains. The only reason was so I could think up all of the things that are impossible. It seems like everything I do just isn't good enough. My award blew by, almost unnoticed. My honours standing seemingly meant nothing. I don't even think I heard "I'm proud of you." or "Congratulations!" I don't even think I heard "Good work." I don't care anymore. What do I want out of life? What life? It was ruined by a series of abusers who stole from me, hurt me, exposed me to traumas I never should have experienced, and told me ridiculous stories such as the one who told me I was haemorrhaging and dying when I started my period, or better yet, the one who told me "Watch out, now you can get pregnant."

My life has been ruined. I couldn't go to a high school with all of my friends because of the reputation that preceded me. I was expected to be a druggie, a slut and stupid. People started calling me names, made assumptions about my traumas, life and choices; I was getting asked out by druggies, the whole works. I hate life! If I could I would kill myself, but I'd hate to think I'd have to go through it all again!

*February 16*th*, 1991. Well, Mom has been really annoying lately. But what really bugs me is when she told me I* could *go to Paris to see my pen pal Val in the summer and then, after I told everyone, she said I* can't, *that we didn't have enough money. Yeah. Why say yes in the first place? Why raise my hopes? What was I going to tell everyone? You see that it was all just a lie. I wanted everyone to be jealous so I made a big deal of it." Um, can you count how many friends I'd have left? Life stinks; at times like this I wish I had leukaemia or something. People would visit me in the hospital. I wouldn't have to see Mom as much. I could keep up my work and I would get flowers and stuff. I feel so sorry for myself right now. I'm going to need to get a scholarship to university so I can leave town! She loves to give me high hopes then just dash them on the rocks.*

Sometimes my adventures are my choosing and sometimes they are experiences forced upon me. So many times it seems I was put in the right place at the right time to deal with someone else's trauma. August 8th, 1991. *I was babysitting and the baby started crying. I went upstairs to get him, came back down and the house was full of smoke. I yelled to the other two kids upstairs to come downstairs as we had to get out of the house. I called my mom (across the street) to call 911 and then come help me. The fire trucks showed up, and the fire-fighters found toast in the oven that had caught on fire. I talked to the kids about fire safety and they enjoyed seeing the fire truck. The parents came home and apologized. The mom was making toast before they left and forgot to turn the oven off.* From very early on, even at the age of 15, I could manage emergencies and function efficiently under intense pressure to ensure physical and emotional safety for others.

For March break we spent all morning deciding on where to go. Just after I tell a couple of people we are doing something that I would like to do, Mom cancels. Whenever I get excited about something, she has to go and cancel it. Why get happy or excited about something when whatever it is won't happen. Why should I show joy if you are just going to destroy it? Why should I become excited if you are just going to cancel it? Why should I show interest if you are just going to throw it away? I promise to become a zombie, show no emotion, think no positive thoughts, so I will feel no disappointment when something I really want doesn't happen; first Christmas, then Paris, now March Break. She suddenly acts like we are best friends. Forget it Mom! *Leave me alone. Whenever I want something or want to do something it seems like you go out of your way to make sure it doesn't happen. From now on I will show no emotion at home and I will become a better person.*

April 15th, 1992. Well, I will be turning 16 in a week and I was going to curl my hair and wanted a practice run. I asked Emily for her curling iron and she said to look downstairs. So I went and looked around in the back room and by mistake found a present. There were three parts: stickers with my name on them, a colouring book, and a zodiac mug like the one Emily got for her birthday. I'll probably be the first person to get stickers and a colouring book for her sweet 16. I don't know what to do. How can I get it across to her that I'm going to be a senior next year? There are only three years left until I go to university. Is this who she thinks I am? Is this what she thinks I like? She is so wrong. Dear God. Please *help me.*

April 22nd, 1992 was my 16th birthday. Evidently, I wrote this in January 1993, after he died, but there were no earlier journal entries regarding it. *I'll never forget the day. Delia was there for me. Our friendship solidified. Dad, I don't believe I can ever forgive you for the things you had done to me. I hate you so much I want to scream, yet at the same time I love you so much I want to cry. I have to live without a father, but do I have to carry around all of this hate, loss and guilt? I know that you did your best with what you had. I deserved better treatment. The things you did ruined a lot of my life including my childhood and my 16th birthday. The memories often invade my mind and thoughts.*

I get so angry I want to hurt you really bad to give back to you what you did to me. I don't know what to do. I wanted to tell you, but I couldn't think of a way to do it. I know you now know my feelings towards you, but still I feel as though all of this emotion is bottled up inside of me. I know it wants to get out. I had hoped with all of my heart, I wanted to believe you had changed, but I couldn't. I hated you. I thought it was wrong for you to treat me this way. I wanted to believe you had become a good person, but when I thought of you in my mind I saw you in total anger coming after us with belts. I have no good memories of you, nothing to remember you by. Every single one is full of hatred. All the good things you did I believe were out of guilt. Everyone is telling me how Emily and I were your pride and joy. Yeah? Well you were the blackness of my past! I wanted to sometimes lose the hatred I have for you. Now all I have of you is memories, and none of them are pleasant. I hate you so much I want to scream, but love you so much I want to cry and I have, but I hate you for putting me through this pain and making me cry.

There was a play that made my birthday memorable. It was a play on abuse. People from the neighbouring high school were there many of my elementary friends present. There was a father who triggered memories of you Dad. In the play he beat his wife and children and totally mutilated a turkey dinner, throwing pieces of it all over, with hateful emotions. So the older brother began to follow his father's footsteps and beat up his girlfriend and sister. I handled most of this with a cold shiver, fighting back tears by biting my lip. But when the guy started to scream he made eye contact with me and held my gaze for about three seconds. I lost it. I grabbed Delia and ran. My eyes met Graham's sitting in the bleachers with Tracy and Colin, watching me run out in tears. My stories and my past, once safe and trusted, were now in a whole new environment. I had new friends. I wanted to grab Graham, Colin and Tracy for all their comfort, history and trust. I had to open up to someone new... Our English teacher saw us, but I didn't care. I felt like I was six years old and that person screaming at me was you.

Delia and I were in the change room. I couldn't stop crying. All the emotion that had built up was now exploding. I couldn't handle this. I had to talk. Thank God the guidance counsellor came in when I wasn't talking yet. Delia insisted that the guidance counsellor we both liked, Mr. Knights, come to talk to us. It never really mattered what she did after that.

I knew I'd never forget how she helped me survive such a traumatic public experience. For this I will always remember the good times we had. I had told Delia almost everything, the pain and suffering I had experienced; she told me I needed to talk to my father about it. I knew I had to but I thought I would have time. I really wanted him to know the pain, the tragic emotional suffering he had inflicted upon me. I wanted him to experience the pain he gave to me.

That night a friend from elementary school, Jessica, called to ask if I heard what happened at the play: some girl went running out in tears. Was she mocking me? "Yeah, it was a crappy performance." I told her.

"Did you know who it was" she asked.

I thought she knew. Colin, Graham and Tracy all saw me run out. "It was me." I responded.

"Shut up." she said, clearly not believing me.

"Seriously, my dad messed us up." I found myself reliving it all over to someone who thought they'd known me for the last five years.

September 20th*, 1992. We were closing up the Hunting and Fishing Lodge my dad was a partner in.* (The word "lodge" still makes me laugh. There was a generator for lights and the fridge. The hand-pumped running water was from the lake and the outhouse was over 20 feet away from the structure. There were two bedrooms both set up with two bunk beds, foam mattresses and everything else was "bring your own.") *I loved going there for the down-to-earth remoteness of it. Barb (dad's girlfriend) took Emily and I for a walk through the forest, talking about what was edible, how to pick up on animal tracks and all that nature stuff, including how to find our way out of a forest. Just as we were heading out, this wicked storm started. The problem was the pontoon plane just took off with Emily and Barb. Dad and I were going to take the boats back to the landing, about a 15 minute ride in good weather. I had planned to drive, but with the storm I questioned my skill. There were too many shallow rocky zones with the water levels in the lake so low. In the narrows, not only did I have to manoeuvre between the rocks, but there* *was that crazy narrow section near the end where I had to work on getting between all the weeds and tree roots! Still in a horrendous thunderstorm, I navigated the motor boat and I only grazed something a few times. There were multiple white outs. Sure, it took almost twice the usual time, but what an adrenaline rush when we made it.* Reflecting back now, I'm glad my last trip to Vanessa Lake was a memorable one, when doubt was conquered and my ability to succeed was reinforced, even when faced with challenging obstacles.

5

A Time to Cry

y father gave me a penny minted in 1919 when I lost my last baby tooth, a molar, in grade seven, 1988. It was a good, long-lasting gift. I often held that penny to remember him. There are so many memories tied up in that coin. The overpowering one is his death.

The tooth dreams continued predicting deaths even after my grandmother. The location and intensity of the tooth relayed the sex and age of the person as well as the type of death. The dreams normally gave me about a week to figure out who it was and prepare for the loss about to occur. My Uncle Mike died and then Uncle Bob (a US Marine) killed himself.

November 27th, 1992. *Crap is about to be unleashed. I just woke up. My mouth hurts. I dreamt I went to the washroom to look in the mirror, and my upper back molar was all bloody and hurt really bad. It looked like it tried to hang on, but fell out in a crumbling bloody mess. I'm filled with intense sadness. Upper back molar – it's a middle-aged man who is going to die a bloody death very soon.*

I found a document that highlighted the best journal entries: *It was December 1992. I was 16. My parents had been separated for quite a few years. I had just gone to my dad's to pick up my mittens for a skating party. His car was in the driveway, there was food on the counter, maybe from today, maybe from last night, thoughts of that tooth dream I had last week were present in my mind. I called out to see if he was here. No answer. I went to check the hand towel in the bathroom, it was dry. Instantly, I knew he was dead. I got my mittens and left. My mom was waiting for me in the car. I told her what I saw and my thoughts that he was gone. We got a call from my uncle and Bob (my dad's best friend), they were concerned. Emily and I were the only ones with keys, so we let them in. We searched the house then called the police to report a missing person. Intuitively I knew where the body was. I told my mom, and she went back with Bob and they found him.*

It all came too soon for most people to handle. The warning dream and the intuition wasn't enough to prepare me for the truth. This must be hysteria. I can't believe it. My father is dead. Why am I laughing? I don't understand. I can't take this seriously. Someone is playing a stupid joke. Now my mother is in on it. I know he is no longer with us, but I'm just not sure I believe it.

The hardest part was telling Billy. I loved my brother. I knew how he'd take it. I doubt I'll ever forget. He came to our house. He was almost six feet tall, with a large frame and straggly hair. He's one of these guys who looks tough. He filled the doorway and had this crazed look on his face. He knew something was going on. "What happened?" he asked in a stern yet frightened voice.

"Billy sit down." *my mom said as she tried to inject some calm into the situation.*

"What happened?" *he persisted.*

"It's Dad..." *she said. Her words came out in a whisper. The silence had not lasted more than a second when my brother entered an unending frenzy. We'd all changed, never to return to what we were.*

"What happened?" *my brother asked. His words bellowed through the house. I couldn't handle it any longer. He was supposed to be strong! If he was falling apart, how could I possibly survive?*

I walked up to him and gave him a hug. "He's dead."

There was silence. No one knew what to say, but we all knew what was coming.

"How?" *he asked. It was hard to tell the tiny voice came from my brother.*

"Billy, no..." *my mom pleaded.*

"Tell me how! I have to know." *he demanded, the urgency in his voice also written all over his face. At this point, Mom broke down.*

"I went back with Bob, and that's when I found him." *she said. The words came out as if they were rehearsed a thousand times in her brain.*

Still my brother persisted. "Where was he?"

"Billy, no..." *she held back the tears.*

"Where was he?" *he asked. Panic was starting to take over.*

"Billy, come on." *she said. You could see her reliving it in her mind.*

"Where was he?" *he insisted. The fear screaming through his words were met with her meek voice.*

"The freezer." *The words had no sooner come out of her mouth before his screaming began.*

"No, no, no, please, God, no!" *he said. He looked like he was about to punch a window. I couldn't help being scared. He wouldn't let us come near him. It took a long time for him to calm down and then he just sat on the front porch and cried. My brother, the strong 24-year-old I had come to depend on, was in pieces and I couldn't help him.*

My radio was still set to wake me up. It was Wednesday December 9th and the alarm seemed coincidently timed with the broadcast: *"… man was found dead in his basement freezer on Tuesday afternoon. Foul play is suspected. Police have not yet released this man's name."* This is what I got to wake up to. Should I throw my radio at the wall? Or should I go to school? Grade 11 math was first period, with Mr. Dubik. I should go to school. The police said we couldn't talk about it. So I simply told my best friend, Delia, that my dad died.

As more information became available to the public, I was sure all my friends knew it was my dad. *The gruesome information was all over the radio and papers. I learned about the hatchet that delivered the deadly blow that killed my father, how his body was tossed in the freezer, likely awaiting disposal. I also learned how heartless teenagers can be. People actually came up to me and said "Hey, was that really your dad who was found in the freezer?" I guess I kind of expected the taunting, being in high school, but I hoped that someone would be able to still treat me like I was their friend, or at least treat me as if I was still human.*

Friday, December 12th, the questioning began. My brother was a suspect and sole beneficiary of the $100,000 life insurance policy. Our house was worth less than that. It was to be expected he'd be investigated. My parents had been separated for years. Billy is the oldest, and the only one of us who was around when my dad started working. Evidently he never bothered updating the policy.

Two detectives showed up to ask each of us some questions. They started with my mom and Emily. We had to stay out of the room until it was our turn. Sergeant Detective Terry caught my eyes first. He was a fresh graduate, likely in his late twenties. He was built, clean cut and more handsome than any TV detective I've seen. My first thought was: "If he's the one asking questions, I might just take my time." He was so nice to look at. Detective Mills, however, was exactly what I thought a detective would be like. He was old, stern, cold and to the point. I wouldn't have survived the session if it weren't for Terry. Not only was he beautiful, he was calming and had these eyes that showed he cared. He used first names. He was so warm compared to Detective Mills, who even in introductions was cold and formal.

The questions began simply. Terry made me a tad more comfortable. Mills got the facts down, asking most of the questions:

"How old are you, Angela?" Mills somehow found a way to say it that implied I was too young to know anything.

"I'll be seventeen in a few months." I quietly replied.

Terry then interjected, "How's school going? Your mom said you were on the honour roll."

Relaxing, I said "Yeah, I'm doing fairly well. I'm going to be the yearbook editor next year and I'm actively involved in the band and theatrix."

"How often did you and your sister go over to your dad's?" he started.

"We usually went every other weekend." I said.

"When was the last time you saw him? Here's a calendar to help you with exact dates." he said as he slid the calendar towards me.

"It was November 28th when he dropped us off." I replied.

"When did you expect to see him next?" he continued.

"The following weekend." I said.

"When did you notice something was wrong?" he asked.

"Well, he was supposed to pick us up on December 5th because he was going away with Bob on Monday. Dad never came to pick us up. We phoned many times, but there was no answer. I had to go and get my mittens for a skating party when I noticed that things were not right. There was food on the counter, his car was in the driveway and the hand towel in the washroom was dry. I told my mom. A few family members were getting anxious and Emily and I were the only ones with keys so we went to let them in." I felt like I was rambling, good thing he interrupted.

"Who's 'them'?" asked Detective Mills.

"Well, um, Bob, my dad's best friend, and two of his buddies and my aunt and uncle." I was starting to feel uncomfortable again.

"What happened when you entered said building?" Mills continued in a monotone voice.

I looked at Terry for some encouragement. "Angela, we need to confirm what other people have said. Your information is important to help us catch the people who did this to your family. Do you want to take a break or shall we continue?"

Terry made me feel as if I actually had power. I could control them. "I'll continue." I said. "Once we entered my dad's house, everyone made their own observations. The fax was unplugged, the VCR was blinking a false time, Dad's shaving kit wasn't in the bathroom and the towels were still dry..."

Terry looked perplexed. "What do you mean by the towels were still dry?" he asked.

"Well, I checked them when I noticed he wasn't there and if he had returned he would have gone to the bathroom and washed his hands or had a shower. So I checked to see if any of the towels had any remnants of moisture. Anyway, I went into his bedroom next, and Emily followed me. His bags were there, open and only half packed. At that point, I counted his guns. Emily and I both realized the same thing. There was one gun missing. We didn't tell anybody there but we both knew something really bad had happened." I said.

I didn't know how much detail I should have gone into with the detectives. Should I have included my thought process? Should I tell them that I believed we were in a mystery novel at that point? But that I already knew the answer based on that dream? Should I tell them my dream? No, I'd stick to the questions they asked.

"I then called my mom to tell her how things were going. We decided to call the police and report my father missing." Everything was so fresh, repeating itself in my mind. I was going crazy. All I wanted to do was forget about it and go on with my life.

"Did anyone go downstairs anytime during the night to the laundry room?" Terry asked, interrupting my thoughts.

"Yes, I wanted to check the entire house before I left." I didn't want to tell them that I knew he was in the freezer.

"I didn't want to leave with any doubt in my mind. It was the only place left. I didn't get in, though. The door was locked, which was unusual. Using a knife I tried to open the lock on the door, but my aunt saw what I was doing and stopped me. She told me not to break in because I'd be destroying the door and any possible evidence. I stopped." I knew it was likely best not to find him with that many people in the house.

The detectives asked a few more questions and then thanked me for my help. Terry told me I was quite perceptive when describing the house then said I'd make a good detective. He commented on how wise it was to count the guns and to feel the towels. I thought it was nice of him to make me feel important. I wondered if any of my information would assist in the arrest of the people that did this to my dad. Terry thanked me, told me to call if I remembered anything else, and they left.

Terry called a few days later to talk to my mom about something she told him. My mom told us she had told them about her dream and the fish with the pattern. It ended up being the pattern of a shoe print.

Emily and I got a call to identify some of the pictures they took of my dad's house. Dan was the Crown Attorney; he lived just down the street from us. His office was everything you'd expect in a Crown Attorney's office. Suddenly he seemed so much more impressive than he did as just a neighbour. He showed us a photo album and asked us to go through it, just to make sure everything in the pictures was normal and where it was supposed to be. I guess we shouldn't have continued flipping the pages. How did we know it was the end of the 'upstairs photographs?' We turned the page and saw the body of my father lying on the cement floor beside the freezer. Blood covered the floor. My dad's blood had soaked all of his clothing. His eyes were closed, red streams running down his face through his beard and down his neck. His hair was clumped together in a dark gooey mass. It looked like his wounds started bleeding again as the blood that had been frozen started to thaw. The picture was instantly imprinted in my memory, to remain forever. He was lying there, dead, with a gaping wound in his head, gorier than any horror movie I've ever seen. I could feel my stomach churning, but my eyes couldn't leave the picture.

"Angela, turn away!" I ordered myself to refocus on something else. But I couldn't. My eyes began to glaze over. I wanted to help him. I wanted to bring him back to life. Take mine; just don't let my daddy die. Not like this. Please God... help him! If you really exist why don't you save him?

I knew nothing could be done. Tears found their way out of my eyes. Dan looked at us and then at the photo album, he saw the picture we were looking at. We were frozen unable to do anything. He reached over and closed the book. He apologized and offered us tissues. Emily and I took time to recover. We then made a silent but understood agreement to never tell Mom what we just saw.

It is December 18th. Christmas was only one week away, but the tension was building in our house. Jennifer (my older sister) moved in with her son and announced she was pregnant. Safety, trust, hope, and anything remotely good is gone. The police are insisting on our silence until the trial, and they even interrupted phone calls: "We told you not to discuss this case." they said.

Life seemed surreal. There were so many fights. It's Christmas, a time of happiness and togetherness. There we were fighting again. Many things were said, hardly any of them our true feelings. I just couldn't handle any more. I went to my room and wrote a poem:

I Miss You.

I can't believe it's been so long,
Since I stood there by your side.
It's been three long hard weeks,
Since I last saw you alive.
I still feel the stabbing pain,
From the last time you said good-bye.
You drove away, had I known then,
I'd have held on and never let you die.
I would have held you in my arms,
Like I long to do today.

If I had you with me just one last time,
I'd never let you go away.
There is an aching pain formed in my head,
And in my heartbeats too.
For every time my heart must pump,
I remember you.
That's how many thousand times a day,
You are in my mind.
So many pictures I see flashed,
So many of them unkind.
I can't believe it happened to you,
I can't believe you're gone.
It hurts today, as I'm told it will,
For ever, ever so long.
But I will not wipe my tears away,
They flow with a painful strive.
It hurts to remember, it hurts to think,
It hurts to be alive.
For every street has a memory,
Every shop a little reminder.
Something that makes me scream out the words,
Please, give me back my father.

Angela, 1992

I cried until the tears ran dry. I didn't think I could cry anymore. Emily had heard me sobbing and came into my room. She was consistently one of the few good things in my life. "What's wrong?" she asked.

"I'm so sick of fighting. We lost dad, isn't that enough? I need you guys right now and all we do is fight. I can't take it anymore. We need to help each other through this. I need you to help me through this." Tears were now streaming down both of our faces. We sat on my bed, holding each other and crying.

The biggest trigger, however, was when we saw our old neighbours at the grocery store. They hugged us and then said "That bastard deserved everything he got!" Wow, could you get more brutally honest? They were right; it was just so hard to hear. Suddenly all the memories came flooding back, all of the crap and abuse my father inflicted. They remembered the calls to the Children's Aid Society, the yelling, screaming, the bruises, the police visits. Maybe it was better he was dead. Their comment resonated with me and maybe everyone else was thinking the same thing. Every time someone spoke, fights were starting. Everything was going wrong. Nobody felt like doing any shopping, decorating, or baking. We all kept to ourselves.

Almost as if my mind did not agree with the puzzle as it presented itself, the dreams explaining his demise continued. On December 19th, 1992 I had the dream for the first time:

> That was the worst and scariest dream I ever had. I was in the car with Emily on our way to visit Dad for the weekend. Mom dropped us off at the front door, but it was locked, so we went around back. We walked along the path beside the house. As we were approached the back of the house, we heard voices. I bent down to look in through the basement window to watch my dad being killed, the axe was raised. That's when I saw her (one of my known abusers); she was standing there watching it. I saw her say "If you really love me you will kill him." to the man with the axe.
>
> She then saw me; her eyes seemed to stare me down. The blunt end of the axe connected with the back of my dad's head, knocking him to the ground. Then, as if his head were a log, the sharp end of the axe was swung at his head and sliced him open. I could see the axe lodged in the back of my father's head. Initial attempts to remove showed it was thoroughly stuck, wedged deep inside his skull. It took the force of a foot, squishing my dying father's head on the ground to get sufficient leverage to pull the blade of the axe out. She then leaned in and said something in the ear of the man holding the axe. He

looked up and his eyes met mine. *Emily and I ran. Weaving in and out of our neighbours' yards and hiding behind bushes, we could hear him running after us. We made it to Billy's. Billy opened the door and saw our faces. He asked, "What's wrong?"*

Then Jennifer stepped out of the back room. "They know." she told him.

Emily and I ran again. We made it home. Mom's van was there. We ran inside to get mom, grab our stuff and get out of town. As we were going up the stairs, we saw the light flashing on the answering machine in Emily's room. "You're too late."

Scared and shivering, our eyes met. "Quickly!" I said with urgency. *We each went to grab clothes. I went to my room, and my mom was in there. She was lying on my bed bloody, her glazed eyes leaving no doubt she was dead. We grabbed the keys and took off.*

Wondering where to go, we headed west. Bob's was far enough away, about four hours. Bob owned a general store, restaurant and motel with his wife. They were there. We told them what happened. They called the police. We sat and drank a hot chocolate. We were safe. I needed a shower, to wash away the horror of the day. They gave us each a loaded hunting rifle and keys to a room. We went to try and calm ourselves before the police arrived. I got in the shower; the water was as hot as I could get it without burning myself. I could feel every sensation. As the hot water poured on me, my mind began to fall apart. Both of my parents were dead and Jennifer and Billy were involved.

"Help!" *Emily's cry broke through the sound of my thoughts and the shower. I grabbed the rifle and a towel and ran out. The axe murderer was on top of Emily, raping her. I shot him. He didn't stop. I shot him again. In the head. Again. In his chest. In the heart. In the face. In the gut. He kept going. Now he was bleeding from all the bullet wounds, dripping blood on Emily. I hit him in the head with the butt of the rifle, throwing him off of her. Nothing could kill him. We fought until we couldn't fight anymore.*

> *Bob and his wife came to assist, their efforts useless. Billy and Jennifer showed up and killed them with a single shot each. My eyes met Emily's, in a defeated helpless gaze. We couldn't win. I woke up in a cold sweat.*

This was one of those dreams that repeated, again and again. Clearly there was a message that I wasn't getting. After the first several times, I started going lucid in the dream. I would recognize it was a dream and try to bypass the beginning to call mom to let her know, get her safe. Avoided Billy's house, went straight to Bob's, gathering as much ammunition as I could, knowing what was going to happen. I could never stop them. This dream continued for two years. It was during my last year of high school when the thought occurred to me that the message behind the dream was not to stop them, but to save Emily and myself and choose a different path. I had to accept that I couldn't stop it. Dad was dead; I felt vulnerable and needed to protect those I could. I needed to get mom out. I needed to get Emily out. I could never figure out if Billy and Jennifer were trying to protect us, why they killed Bob and his wife, if they had Dad killed or what their knowledge about the events was. I know I had too many flashbacks and I was younger than both of them. Who knows how much they remember or what was done to them.

My stories became secrets and I went into survivalist mode. The best solution was to run away where no one could find me. My goal was to leave town to keep myself safe.

I think what sucks most is that I'm left with so many horrible memories. He was just starting to change. I would have loved to have had a good relationship with him. I would have loved to have forgiven him. I would have loved to hear him say he loved me, just once. Almost in a panic, I started going through every card he had given me over the years, hopeful I'd find something indicating he cared. Deflating a bit with each card I opened, I spiralled deeper and deeper. Did he love me? Trying to justify he cared enough to give a card didn't offer any peace. Every card I had from him, my birthdays, Christmas, was simply signed "Dad."

March 20th, 1993. Well, Delia's party was not exactly planned but it was still a party to remember. I met Nyles. I guess I shouldn't have continued on for so long, but it began to be enjoyable. I didn't really care what he thought of me, because I was only flirting with him in attempt to elicit a response from Levi. But then there's the other part of me who remembers telling him all the information. I told him a lot about my past and my life and was talking on a deeper level than I normally do, none of that superficial garbage.

During the night (we stayed up all night) we talked about many things. At one point his hand was up the back of my shirt and he found a place on my back where I was ticklish and his hands were virtually wandering except he never actually got to anything. Well he kept pushing my head towards his head with his mouth open. After a while I bluntly said "Look I don't exactly want your tongue in my mouth at this moment and there is no way mine is going in yours." He tried to cover up, but he looked rather astonished and stared at me with an odd look for a while. Finally he said it was the first time he had ever been rejected.

Later on we were talking about being ticklish. He was extremely, ticklish. Very rarely am I actually ticklish.

"Yeah but before it was different, you were uncomfortable." he said.

"No I wasn't," I responded, "I just met you and I didn't really want to kiss you because I don't know what we'll be like tomorrow. I don't know if I'll ever even see you again." At this point it got awkward.

Time passed then he told me "I want to ask you something but you have to promise not to get mad." Then he decided it was a stupid thing to ask.

It went on like this for a while and finally I said "Now you've gotten me curious as to what this question is, so would you just ask it?"

"Are you a virgin?" he paused, "You don't have to answer that, you can slap me if you want."

I didn't understand what the big deal was. I knew he'd gotten Bobby pregnant, so clearly he wasn't. I told him "Yes, I am."

He seemed surprised. *"You are the first in a long time."* he said.

I said *"I haven't done anything because I never want to be compared to Jennifer, and if I had sex I would have felt I was more like her than ever."*

"Why are you so careful about what your mom thinks of you?" he asked.

"Whenever I upset her she compares me to Jennifer." I said.

Then he said something that made me think, *"You won't always be able to be mommy's little girl."* Hmmm, was I preserving my virginity for her or for me? To me making out isn't *"for fun"* it's a connection with another person, wanting them to be in my life. I was only flirting with Nyles to bother Levi.

Morning came around, not that I could have slept. I was more curious as to what I should do and if I actually liked him or just used him. I was upset with Levi. I was ready to make a move before I heard what he did. Now I'm unsure as to if I really like either of them.

March 24th I talked to Bobby today about Nyles seeing as we are going out on Friday… I wanted to know more about him. Most of the stories were not good. He has told me many times that this was his past and no longer who he is. He often asks if I trust him. I don't know what to say, I don't know enough about him to trust him. I feel bad to say this but it's true.

April 3rd. Nyles and his father took me out for breakfast, then Nyles and I were dropped off at the theatre. The movie was ok, I guess. We kissed. I definitely was not as ecstatic as when kissed by Neil, but I felt like it was totally natural. We were staring at each other and it just sort of happened. We walked home holding hands. When I am with him I feel so at ease, like I don't have to put on a show and I just have to be myself.

Happy stinking birthday! Yippee, April 22nd and I am sick, really sick. I saw once more that wonderful sheet lying on my desk, telling me, screaming out that I have to go to court for my dad. How sweet for me to be here with this mess.

Then there was my wonderful day at school. Oh yes! I learned that I will again have to appear in court for the wonderful incident of being *rear-ended by Shawn when he pushed my mom's van right through the intersection. Fine, even if I didn't have my left signal on (which I did), the car in front of me did! Can I really have two subpoenas for the same day? I called the city court to tell them I couldn't attend as I was subpoenaed for the same period at a provincial level for a murder trial. Who would have thought my 17th birthday could be worse than my 16th?*

Emily told me that she had a dream about her tooth falling out all bloody and all her hair being cut. (Meaning we were about to have another bloody death, but it would reduce worries. Is that possible?) *I wonder if the guy who did it will be killed before the trial. I hope it's not another family member. I had a dream of Mom being killed. I need to believe it is fear and not that she is the next victim. I'm so ready to scream.*

I went to the drama room and did. I screamed and I screamed and I screamed. Then I didn't want to go home, so I went to Delia's. Then I got bitched out because I'm never at home. I guess those five hours of homework last night didn't count. Thanks for making my day so much better. Not. Hope my next birthday doesn't compete for the last two winners of the worst birthday ever award.

May 10th. I drove out to the trailer park to see Nyles. We went for a walk and sat by the river. He told me that one day we would make love. We lay there for a while kissing and just being next to each other. I think I love him. He said there were things he would stop if they occurred (guess he didn't want to get another girl pregnant). I asked like what? He didn't really reply, except that he wanted an example situation. I then went to unbutton his Jeans. We ended up going back to his place and his friend Steve came over and I listened to them play guitar for a while. They sound so good.

Nyles parents got him tickets to the Jeff Healey concert May 11th as a birthday present. It was a school night but Mom let me go. It was so good! My favourite song was Angel Eyes, *from* See the Light. *I loved it!* It's strange how every time I hear that song I think of him and that moment of eye contact we shared during that song. I think it was the first time I felt completely absorbed in a moment and filled with love. It is one of those memories that seems to pause time as the feelings of love and happiness fill me again.

On Monday May 13th, 1993, we started preparing ourselves for the trial. Defending the accused was one of the best lawyers in town and this was his last case before retirement. Dan brought in my family to show us the court room and gave us a brief outline of what he was going to ask us. I wasn't allowed to sit in on the trial until after I had gone up on the stand. I read about most of what was happening in the newspaper, but I wanted to know more.

May 14th. Today was a really diverse day. I left class to see the student counsellor. Levi was in there, but he let me talk. In front of Levi, I spoke of all my problems, looking at him every once in a while. I felt like it was wonderful progress. Also I made awesome eye contact! I phoned him and left my number. Most importantly, he called back. I wanted to tell him so much...so many things...but Delia was over and killing my courage. Then Delia, Ian, Nyles and I went to the movies. Delia dared me to eat raw garlic, so I did. Nyles was upset but I didn't care. I just hoped that Levi would call back. Levi makes me fluttery, my heart flying around, my mind swirling, my stomach full of butterflies and a tingling sensation throughout my whole body. With Levi I would be happy emotionally and physically. Why can't I have both?

Today was my day to get up on the stand, Tuesday May 21st. I was as nervous as could be. Dan only asked one question I wasn't expecting. "What was your brother's reaction when he was told what happened to your father?" *The emotions were so powerful I didn't know if I should answer. My lips were already quivering when I opened my mouth to speak.*

"He freaked..." *I started crying. All the memories of his reaction filled my mind.* "He was so upset. I didn't know what to do. He scared me."

The last words were hardly audible when Dan said, "No more questions. Does the defence wish to cross-examine?"

They got me some water and gave me time to stop crying before he began. I'm not sure if that was supposed to be supportive for my brothers' case or just to put me in tears to minimize the questions from the defence, but I believe Dan was trying to protect me. As it was, I was only asked a few questions. As much as I tried to attend court after my appearance, it was too much to watch.

Terry tried to make it easier on us. He would sit with me and Emily and be playful. On water day (at school we'd bring water guns and balloons to school and play outside activities most of the afternoon) Terry actually got into a water fight with us in the court room. He sprayed Emily with water using a small water gun. Emily and I had to retaliate. He looked around to see who saw then said "I didn't know it had water in it."

I'm not sure if he was trying to cover himself, but Emily and I needed his light-hearted approach. As bearable as he tried to make it, court became too emotional; I couldn't watch the trial. I stopped reading the paper. I was sick of crying. I went to school like a zombie, did my work, came home and went to sleep. I was so emotionally drained; sleep was all I was capable of.

The accused was supposed to get up on the stand Thursday May 23rd, but he couldn't because he had "a tummy ache." Friday morning he changed his plea to guilty and was sentenced to life in prison with a chance of parole in 12 years. I guess it gave closure to all of this misery, but I still felt empty. It left too many questions. A guy willing to take an axe to someone couldn't go on the stand because of a "tummy ache"? How could any one person pick up my dad as a dead weight and lift him up into a chest freezer? It just leaves too many questions. Who helped? Who is he protecting? Did he even do it, or is he taking the fall to protect himself? Did someone threaten him and force him to take the fall for the murder?

At seventeen, I was forced to deal with more than anyone I had ever met. I lost my childhood long ago. My father's death made me lose so much more. All the love, trust and hope I ever had for a future was crushed when I realized all the things I would never do. Each step I take and every plateau I reach I realize how alone I really am. Somehow, it seems as if life would be easier if I didn't take any more steps. Still, I continue with a *painful strive. I have to prove to the world that even though I had endured my childhood, my father was murdered and I temporarily lost all hope that I can continue. I know this is going to be a difficult journey. I wonder how I can lessen the impact of this trauma.*

May 26th, 1993. I broke up with Nyles. I couldn't stand going out with him anymore. I still want to hold him and be near him. I am glad I went out with him. He made me feel sure of myself. He made me actually like myself again. He improved my self-confidence and I know now that I can get a guy when I want one. He made me feel a lot better about myself. My heart is just no longer in it.

Our teacher hosted a band party on June 6th. I don't know why we started playing truth or dare; I needed to get my mind off on my stuff. I was sitting next to Kevan. He was a willing participant in anything people dared me to do to him. The first was to suck his toe. Clearly we looked comfortable with each other. Emily said Kevan and I looked good together then dared me to French kiss him. After the kiss we held eye contact. Kevan then leaned in and said "That was my first."

I smiled, still enjoying the moment. "Practice could be fun and helpful." I said.

Encouraging a new direction for our relationship, he said "Ok."

Wednesday June 30th, 1993. I'm in Paris! There was a guy on the plane who was chatting with me about being away from home.

"I'm still in denial." I responded.

He said "It will hit you, hard, right here." He put his hand to his heart.

So now at Val's I'm with a family, in a family, and yet I feel so alone. He was right. It just hit me. I'm not going to see anyone for three weeks. I feel so alone, so isolated, unknown. Everyone was getting ready for bed. I went to the window for comfort in the sky. As I looked out the window, at the very first star I saw, a blue halo formed, and as it enlarged I watched in awe. I wonder how many others in the world got to watch the very same sky. How many saw the beauty, the wonder? I have never seen a star enclosed in a ring of blue. It proved to me that I am never truly alone; the sky connects me. It was a timeless gift from God.

August 5th. I went out with Kevan tonight. It was weird having to sit there and not do anything. It was definitely weird. We started as friends, dared to do more, did more, and then nothing. I feel attracted to him. I've known him for so long that, I feel like I know almost everything about him. But lately I've been thinking, why not make a move? And then I begin to think about various reasons why I shouldn't and a few why I should. He's a great guy and easy to talk to, he listens, and he's always there. But he's so annoying at times and I just feel frustrated. I don't know what to do, but I did have fun tonight!

On August 12th, 1993, we went to a park near the falls to watch the big meteor shower. It was a nice night with a clear sky. I sat on the swing, swinging and staring up at the night sky. This was my first good meditative moment, feeling grounded and connected to the universe. I lay down on the ground, feeling the warmth of the summer through it, the softness of the night breeze against my skin and the sky above me filled with shooting stars. This is one of the moments I return to for good grounded meditations. Feeling small and insignificant and yet privy to the majesty of an amazing night sky and the best meteor shower I had ever seen.

Kevan and I hung out a lot, went to semi together and he surprised me with a big box of chocolates for Valentine's Day. Kevan and I went back to being "friends" one day when we were having a deep conversation and he shifted it by saying "I wanted you to be the first to know." he told me. "When I'm around you I can be myself. You make me comfortable with who I am as a person and now I feel I no longer have to hide my true self." He was going to announce to the world he is gay.

6

Growing Up

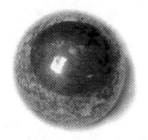

This ball bearing fits perfectly inside the metal ring Delia gave me. It's amazing how many memories can be brought back and the energy contained within metal. This ball bearing was given to me after an accurate target practice with its twin. Holding it now in my hand gives me such pleasure. Why did I crave revenge for what I believe to be unjust acts done to me? Is it power? Is it creating a balance? The token was given to me to remind me about balance: both strength and fragility, and power and helplessness. It is a reminder to treasure moments because everything can change so fast. A reminder that some people will stand with you, to work through whatever issues may be at hand. It was the first time anyone stood up for me, reminding me that I didn't have to be the victim.

September 1st after coming back from France, Delia and I got into a big fight about everything and nothing. She had spent a lot of time with Nyles in my absence. He and I broke up after my dad's trial and I was ok with it for the most part until, she called, upset, and gave me the full story about everything they have done. Our relationship changed. I felt like an outsider because of my dad's death and then I lost my best friend and my boyfriend and felt even more alone. Many people who were critical to my life stopped the regular day chatting, and interactions became rare. It was crazy going back to school; realizing friendships were changing as levels of trust and communication impact interactions and modify relationships.

One friend unexpectedly decided to get closer. *Today when I was walking home, I saw him leaving the school, moving quickly in my direction as I turned the corner, so I slowed my pace. I was expecting him to catch up and decided not to turn around. I heard his footsteps approaching. "Boom, you'd have been dead by now."*

I turned and smiled, "I knew you were following me."

We walked to my place, dropped off my bag, then walked towards his place. We ended up at a park on the swings and talked for over an hour. I looked at my watch "It's time for you to go home." he said.

I got up to leave, he followed me. "Hmm, you know you're walking in the wrong direction right?" I said.

He smiled, "I was just being nice, thought I'd walk you back and then go to the school to talk to a friend."

"So," I said, "the point of the walk with me was to waste time?" I was pushing the limits, wanting him to tell me it was more than that.

"No," he said, "the point was to go home, but we walked instead." Somehow he ended up thanking me. It was a playful, deep and amazing

afternoon. We started hanging out during our spare period, we held hands, and we kissed, but when it came down to it, he wasn't ready to be public about our relationship.

I started my classes on February 16ᵗʰ, 1994. *I had wanted to learn to scuba dive as long as I could remember. I went with Sue* (a friend and band mate). We were scheduled to do our first open water dive for certification shortly after the ice broke. *It was so cold! I had to do a regulator clear and I was so cold I couldn't feel my regulator against my mouth. It took three attempts against my face before it was actually in my mouth! I performed all requirements for certification. I loved every minute of it! Scuba diving was everything I dreamed it would be. I had always longed to float weightlessly, observing life otherwise unobservable. Of course it was much more enjoyable in warmer water, but I was eager to start as soon as I could.*

February 28ᵗʰ, 1994. There was a production in the auditorium. During the second half of the performance, this guy came out and talked to us for a while, he told us he has AIDS. He talked some more then we asked him questions. He was asked a lot of difficult ones; they were answered seriously but light-heartedly. I could tell that he felt the need to go up on stage and tell people what it was like. I felt for him. Afterwards, he invited people with more questions to go and talk to him. When I got close up I melted. He saw me and made eye contact. He finished with the previous person, then when he looked at me, I asked, "What did you do about those you had sex with before testing positive for HIV?"

"I didn't have any partners before I tested at age 21." he responded.

As my gaze was held I felt his essence entering my brain. Yes, he was there, deep in my mind, his gaze penetrating my soul. "What is it like knowing you aren't going to – that you won't be around forever?"

He looked slightly hurt, and I immediately regretted asking. But he sensed this, I'm guessing, as he pondered for a moment. Then the smile returned. "Well guess what?" he said.

"What?" I responded.

"You're not going to be around forever either." he told me.

"I know but still…" I said, struggling. "Your life is more – death is more defined."

He responded quickly, understanding completely. "What I do is live for today. Tomorrow will never come and it's painful to think about. Even your own future – how can you be sure? And the past, well; that is even more painful." he said as he continued entering my mind with his eyes. Something changed. I felt different.

Suddenly I felt consumed by energy and purpose. "Can I see your hand?" I asked.

He held it out to me. "What are you doing?" he queried.

"I just wanted to see your life line." I told him, his hand in mine, his warmth and energy filling me.

"And how does it look?" he said, looking way too deep into my soul.

"You are going to live to be old." I replied. His life line went all the way to his wrist.

"Some people think 27 is old." he said seemingly trying to convince himself.

"But it's not," I told him, "there are still things I'm sure you want to do, places you want to see."

"People can and do die at 20. I'm glad to have made it to 27." he said. Wow. To live for today, purposefully meaning to enjoy each day, to wake up and say I'm glad to be here: that was my new goal. I would have my long term goals, but treasure opportunities as they present themselves. Who knows how long any of us have here?

It's March 1st, 1994, and I lost the purpose and determination from yesterday. I feel alone, like no one understands me. I am in a world of my own. There are people around me, but there is something weird about it. It's like I am invisible, yet they see me, like I'm mute, yet I can talk. At least they hear me; I don't know if I do. Am I deaf? But I hear voices. I believe I exist in a different dimension, on the other side of a clear glass enclosure, that others can walk through and every so often someone does. I feel as if they actually understand me, but they leave. I try to follow but I am trapped by the glass. I am alone. I can feel that it must be dark out, although I cannot see. I am blind. Wait. I can feel the sun, beating down on me. I can touch it...so I believe. Wait. What was that? Someone has put a blanket over my cage. I am being moved. Transported? Where? How?

I flash into a party. Hey, it's for me. There are all these people who think they are my friends. Everyone I know! But why aren't they talking to me? Where am I? I am just observing, yet I hear my name. They are talking about me. The rest is muffled. I'm not here. There. I'm not at the party. But? Where am I then? Does anyone know? I am alive...but where...when...I know I exist in both mind and body because when people try to push me around I feel them on my cage. This isn't a body. I feel trapped.

What makes others think they are better than me? Is it because they have a boyfriend? Maybe because they are not virginal? Maybe it's because they don't waste time doing homework, or maybe it's because I have no drugs in my system. Maybe they just have an ego problem and feel the need to put me down! But they are not better than I. For I am virginal, with no piercings or tattoos, and drug free. I don't need acid to forget my problems. I feel pure and it fills me with a good feeling.

I feel suddenly overcome by superiority. I have risen above the crowd. I am 17 going on 38. I was forced to grow up quickly and had to experience things I don't think I should have had to. People now ignore me because of this. I am not equal to them. I have grown up. I have learned things: meanings, purposes. I have watched people die and watched others born. Life. I have seen the beginning; I have seen the end. I don't fear death and I never have. I welcome death as a chance to be removed from Earth into God's open arms. For only God truly understands who I am.

Why did you stay?

If you did not love me, why did you stay?
Why did you play with my feelings that way?
Couldn't you tell me, just straight out, goodbye?
I do have feelings, but I wouldn't have cried!
You think you're so special, so cool, so brave...
I want you to know I'll never visit your grave!
One day now, soon, I will get my revenge...
And I promise to you, your road will then end.
You will be alone, not a friend in the world!
Everything near you, it all will just curdle.
Like milk when rotten, to be thrown down the drain...
Not nothing, not no how, nor anything sane,
Will ever in its life time visit your lane,
Because if they do they all will be slain!
I don't understand why you did this to me.
But you will understand how it hurts.
YOU WILL SEE!!!!!!!!!!!!

Angela, 1994

I shouldn't have submitted that poem for class. April 6th 1994, they sent me to see a therapist. He showed me card tricks that I easily deciphered and which he told me "You are smart."

"I'm not here because I'm stupid. I'm here because I'm depressed." I said.

He tried to diagnose me as paranoid schizophrenic. He didn't believe I had lived through what I had, so I brought in a bunch of newspaper clippings about my dad's murder, my mom finding him, my brother being a suspect... He was in disbelief. "You mean it's all true?" That was the end of that. My therapy required the therapist believe me.

After reading that journal entry, I called to request my records. My favourite entry was the last one. He had done two evaluations on me and was working on a diagnosis. He wrote:

> Persons with similar profiles tend to be somewhat hostile and have difficulty expressing negative emotions appropriately. They tend to be rebellious, adventurous, self-centred and may engage in acting out or antisocial behaviour. Conflicts with authority figures and difficulties in interpersonal relationships are common. Such persons tend to be suspicious and distrustful.

As accurate as this currently feels, combined with the disbelief in my stories, I can see how the discussion of paranoid schizophrenic never made it into the notes. He did, however, in our first meeting comment "She gives the impression of being attractive, alert and of average to above-average intelligence."

It's April 27ᵗʰ, 1994. I don't know why I'm crying. Maybe this is what it is like to be 18. I have so much anger built up inside me I feel like I'm going to burst. No, it's not so much anger, but loneliness and fear. I found a fellow band member in the band room bathtub. She had slit her wrists. She found out she was adopted. The idea that her birth mother didn't want her left her feeling unlovable, so she slit her wrists. I found her, still conscious, bloody, but not in life-threatening danger. I called the office, and they sent down the school nurse and counsellors. I don't get it. She has two parents who chose her and have been good to her. We talked for a while about why life sucks so much. Not that it is a competition or anything, but my life sucks so much worse than hers. I don't want to live anymore either. I wish I was dead. There is nothing for me in this world. There is nothing that I should live for. Everyone I love dies, or screws me over. I'm sick of death. I'm sick of life. I'm sick of emotions.

A person has to know that they are loved, at least by someone. They have to have physical contact with other people. I have no one. I need human contact. Or, maybe I don't need it anymore. I'm so past all that. My wall is built. But the higher it gets, the harder it will fall. My head hurts. I need to stop thinking. But I can't. There is too much I need to get out of my head. Then, maybe then, I can be free.

Free…what a word. If only I could be free. Free of pain, heartaches, headaches, loneliness and memories. If one thing hurts the most it is all those memories. They haunt me so much, when asleep and awake. I had a dream about my dad. I wanted to die, to follow him and get off of this horrible world called Earth. Why am I even here? Do I have a purpose? What have I done to deserve so much pain?

I hate crying. I hate feeling this way. I need to get out of this place. I want to die. I can't finish this life. This is not life, this is hell. I need to leave, to get away from everything. I thought time alone would help. It doesn't. Being alone only gives me extra time to think and when I think, I am not free. I feel the bars clamp down on me as burning needles are being pushed into my mind, heart and soul. I haven't a soul left. It was stolen years ago. If I did have it, I'd trade it for just a moment of pure happiness, where nothing could remind me of the pain and trouble I've experienced. Just for a moment so I could always remember what it feels like for that moment, I would be willing to trade my soul, anything I have, anything I own. For that moment, my mind could linger with the feeling of freedom and answer my prayer. Alas, I will never be gifted with a moment such as this and I am forced to work out all of my problems.

"If I try to stop thinking of the past, what will that do? " I ask myself. I feel hopeless, like nothing will help.

"Come on Ang, you can do this, go logical. You want love?" A voice was now speaking to me. "Clear yourself of hate."

"But how?" Tears were streaming down my face.

"You have to free the part of your brain that is holding on to all of the pain, free it so you never have to feel the misery of the past in the present time. To do this you must enter your brain." Are these really my thoughts, or are they being imposed on me?

So I try. Counting backwards from 100, I exhale with each number, visualizing myself going down a set of stairs. Three, two, one, zero. At the bottom of the stairs, I open a door leading to many halls. I feel myself being pulled to a door at the end. I open the door and find a small child. She is sitting on a bed crying, woeful and forlorn. I recognize this child; she is me. I take her by the hand and tell her we are leaving.

"Where are we going?" she asks in her meek voice.

"I'm taking you to a place where we will no longer feel pain." I hold on to her hand. She is so small and timid.

As we walk, everyone gathers, screaming horrible words at me.

"You are so stupid!"

"You are worthless!"

"You are unlovable!"

"You'll never amount to anything!"

"You can't escape us!"

I see all of their faces. I know what each one of them did to me. I don't feel angry. I just keep walking.

"We will be ok." I tell this small helpless girl at my side. "We will be ok."

At the end of the hall, I take her to a door. We enter. There is silence. All those voices, all those people, they are behind us now.

"I know this place," she says as she turns to me, "it is my heart."

Tears streaming down my face, I say "I love you." I tell her the words I needed to hear so badly. "I will always love you and I will always protect you. You will be safe here." I said as I hugged her, my inner child.

Reading those words now, tears stream down my face again and I wonder…was the purpose of this journey to now set her free? I'm not afraid anymore! Fear trapped me for years, binding me from wrong, directing me to right, forcing me to run away and free myself. Years of therapy later, and the answers were in me all along. It started with the dreams, voices and the self-talk, finding a purpose…finding a destination…wanting nothing more to be free from the pain of oppression. My life is now an open book. I now understand and adhere to the wisdom I had at 18. I was stuck, but I made it through the darkness. Now, reabsorbed in my writings I learn how far the voyage truly was.

October 5th, 1994. What was that about? Delia bothers me!!!! But alas, I need to reaffirm that I am more of a person than she. I saw it as acting civilized I just offered to help; she saw me as a lonely person for whom she is the last hope. Um, no, I don't want to be friends, but I don't want to be enemies either.

Well, I'll just hold my head up; I know I am better than that. I know where I've been, where I'm going and how I'm going to get there. The weird thing is that no one knows me anymore, who I am or what I've become. Life is changing and I am left contemplating my life and altering it accordingly.

I have been through many awful things in my life and handled them all. I am stronger than anyone I know. I know that anything I do will be enough to get me where I'm going and I will have fun – as soon as I leave this place. I am not running away from my problems; I have dealt with them and ready to move on.

We were all a little on edge. Emily and I got $9000 from my father's estate to put towards our education, so my mom decided she could afford to take us to Florida for the holidays. *Well, I don't know if that helped, but it explained life to me.*

That vacation was supposed to clear my brain, but memories seem to be dependent on the company, because all alone I am fine. I need to tell, to talk, to relate what I saw, and ease the pain. I need to be comforted, held, loved, told that everything will be fine and then believe it. I love meditating. I'm leaving; my pain will be dealt with before I go. I'm afraid to be alone. "Can I take somebody with me?" I ask.

"No," the voice says, "you must travel by yourself to show your independence. You will only be alone for a short while, to prove to yourself and others that you can stand on your own two feet. At times you will feel alone and lost, but it is all part of the path. You choose your own path."

Then I hear "It's not a sad thing." It was a line from the movie Made in Heaven. It seems that there is a plan. I'm so tired though.

Yeah, Ok

Snowy white clouds and a soft covered ground,
Love is here, it is all around.
For someday, not known, I will see the end,
The troublesome moments together will blend.
Fogginess will come to me on the hillside,
Meet me with open arms; take me over the hillside,
I am lost, so lost, lost by the hillside,
And there I will die.
Help! Help! Find me within,
Such troublesome moments; please find me,
And wake me up from this bad dream called life.
Because I'm crazy, I'm insane,
I need mental help to clear my brain.
I'm crazy, I'm insane.
But I need you.
I need you to help me breathe,
I need you to hold me tight,
I need you to close my eyes,
And make the stars shine really bright.
Because I'm crazy without you,
And crazy I'll stay,
Until time can change my mind.
  Angela, 1995

I don't know if that poem is enough to summarize my thoughts right now. I was thinking as I stepped out of my body and watched Emily and I correspond in band from an omniscient point of view. Many people observed us, perhaps with envy. It's definitely odd. Will I be losing a part of myself in her when I leave? Or am I setting myself free? I began a new life when I moved to this school. True, I did know a few people, but I made new friends. Friendships to last a lifetime…well, maybe one or two of the friendships may last. But university, I'm told, is where it all begins. All my applications have been submitted.

The time has come to carry myself to new worlds. I have new areas to explore and new ideas to discover. I will go willingly, but there will always be a part of me that will remain on the school playground forever.

7

Saying Good Bye

he microchip was from my international diving card. To me it represents expanding, exploring and standing on my own. There is a second keepsake for this chapter however, and that was the Swiss Army logo which always triggers thoughts of a friendship I came to treasure. It was interesting to review journal entries and realize how many there are about some people and how few about others. Amongst many entries of fleeting crushes there seemed to be consistent entries about this boy Alistair. He started out as a band mate, but entries of him remained constant and showed a growing and changing relationship

January 1995. This is the final entry for this journal. The semester has come to an end and a segment of my life has passed. Only one semester of high school is left for me, and it's my last winter in this city. A difficult step is ahead of me, and it's a frightening one at that. I don't know how deep and truthful I should get in this, but I have been thinking. What was the deeper significance of him asking "Do you like me?"

"Yes." I freely say I like him, but I wonder what my response meant to him and why I didn't ask the same question. Maybe it's because... I don't know. Maybe because I know he likes me. I don't "like him" like him, but I do like him and I know he feels the same about me.

I listen to Alistair's dreamy voice as I fall asleep talking to him on the phone. It is so calm and relaxing; I wish I could reach out and hug him. He hasn't done anything stupid recently and that movie was good. Now he's seen my room and mom let him stay after she had to leave for work because the movie was still on. I know he likes other girls and he knows I like other guys, but the time we spend together is time I treasure.

Time. I mention it frequently, how it passes, and the meaningful experiences that occur in it – the love, trials and tribulations that one must endure. People say time is money, but I believe it is also these people who never stop to look around and notice what's really happening around them. Imagine going through life led by some driving force and never allowed to experience the joys of observing the wilderness contained in this vast expanse called Earth. How do we define a speck? A dot could be me on a map of this town, a town on a globe, the size of Earth twinkling within the Milky Way, or the galaxy itself in the vast expanse of space.

So, I ask myself "Is my life truly important?"

I hear "Yes."

"But why?" I ponder. Why would one person in a world so insignificant hold value?

"You are the only one like you." the voice responds. *It's kind of scary. An average life is about 82 years. I have completed almost 19 years. Within eight months I'll be in university, living under a whole new set of rules, fending for myself, living with strangers. Will I fit in? What will my friends be like? Will I remain a 'quiet shy type' for a year or will my more spazzy behaviour shine through?*

It is February 10th, 1995. *Alistair came over and we worked on calculus. After, we went upstairs and played on the computer. It's weird being around him. Don't think I don't like it, that's not what I'm saying, it's just different. Different from any other relationship I've had with a guy. Sure, I still feel emotions creeping through my mind and body at times, but it's different. Once, he asked, "Why don't you call me more often?" I had no answer, but now that I think about it, I was trying to protect myself from slowly falling for him. Normally when I talk on the phone, if the conversation dies, I get bored quickly. I think Alistair is one of the only guys whom I can be on the phone with without an active conversation, and still be deeply intrigued by just breathing patterns and my own racing thoughts.*

After the movie, I drove him home. He invited me in, so I went. He showed me his main floor and his dog. We played a game of chess. As I was leaving, it was awkward. Many emotions began to run through me and I envisioned the picture from an observer's point of view. We were standing at the doorway. What do I say? What do I do? I want the hug. I want my Valentine moment. Do I initiate? Unwillingly, I forced myself to simply walk out of that door.

February 19th. Oh, how I love it when that happens. I heard a knock at the door, and not expecting it to be anyone interesting I answered it. I saw Alistair standing outside my house. The house was a mess. I should have tidied up.

I opened the door and he entered the porch "I was just wondering if –" his voice trailed off.

"You want my calculus notes?" I offered.

"Well, yeah, that too, I guess." he said as he continued into the house. I went upstairs, got my notes and stuff, because I needed them too. I let him copy them. He sat on the couch.

"Move over." I said, as I sat where there was the least space, between him and the edge of the sofa. We were right next to each other. Both his leg and side were touching me. He began copying out my notes, then asked about the "sex quiz" I was giving him the night before on the phone, so I got the magazine. At one point, we were just sitting there as he was copying out my notes inches from me, and he turned, looking at me.

"Say something." he said.

"Like what?" I responded.

"Well then, ask me something, ok, well, I don't know, do something." His intent was unclear yet suggestive.

"Anything?" I asked.

"Um, ok..." he continued.

I looked at him, inches from me. Wanting what I knew I shouldn't. My feelings were mounting. All I had to do was lean forward. "Sorry, I can't."

My head started screaming. Why? Why can't I do what I want? Time passed. It was 6:45pm and I commented on the time. He said he had to go because his parents needed the car. He offered me my pen, but as I tried to take it, he held on, and pulled it back forcing our hands to touch, many times. He was so playful, light-hearted. I love his eyes. I needed to say something. I should have said something. It's weird when I'm sitting so close to him. I want to do something, but I think about it and it seems like there are only two possible directions. It would either destroy our friendship and we'd become uncomfortable around each other and stop talking or it would lead somewhere and we'd become amazingly close with so much potential and then I'd have to leave. I feel like I'm giving up before I even try, but I can't stop myself from flashing forward.

I had an amazing conversation with Alistair last night (March 3rd). There were no pauses. I just feel like he understands me. Everything came out: the nightmares I used to have about dad, all the cruel things he did, the words of hatred I screamed into my pillow as I cried and prayed for it all to stop. Alistair listened. He can hear my stories. It's weird. I could be irritated with him beforehand and not want to talk to him, but as we talk he calms me greatly.

March 21st. We talked on the phone tonight for hours. It's hard to believe how much I like him. When we talk over the phone I wish he was here beside me so the comfort would be complete. Last night we were talking about sex. He asked who I would sleep with if I had the chance. I told him "I would have to build up to it; I couldn't just say yeah, I'd sleep with this person."

Then I reversed the question. He rhymed off a few people, said "you," paused, then rhymed off a few more. It was awkward, but nice. Then he commented "We aren't compatible."

"How can you say that?" I asked. "You say it every so often then the next night we talk again for hours." Maybe it's true, maybe that's why it never goes anywhere.

Then he asked "Do you know what I was thinking? There is something there... but..." he trailed off.

"We both like too many other people." I said.

"Well, not exactly," he said, "it's more because neither of is looking for a serious relationship."

Then it came down to me. It's face to face we never seem to relate as well. I didn't say it out loud but it was true. I like his eyes, but I'm not really attracted to him, yet on the phone I feel so comfortable with him. I don't know, perhaps we'll go out but there are little things about him that bother me in person that would keep us from getting serious. It's just so awkward at times. I'm sure it's my restraint and not being true to my feelings that allows for the inconsistent interactions. I don't know how to put it in words.

I don't know what to do. I can't stop thinking about Alistair. Sure he often has some negative retort for almost every compliment or positive remark I make, but then again I do the same thing, not wanting him to know how much I really care. I've been thinking about him so much recently that it's overpowering. I really enjoyed singing to him last night, because I know he enjoyed it. I recorded myself singing to observe how I sounded and I sounded pretty good. To think it all began with my slow tired voice softly singing to him late one night. Following that was the first true compliment he gave me, besides the one about my hair. The next time we spoke he said I had a voice that could make someone cry. From then on I've sung to him a few times. It seems that he enjoyed it. I'm glad he did because I enjoy singing to him. I enjoy him. Why don't we get along as well in person as we do over the phone? I don't want to talk to him again so soon. I'll wait for him to call because if I keep talking to him, like we have been I know I'd fall for him. I don't want to, so I'm forcing a restraining order on myself. Wait for him to call before you talk to him next.

I waited three days for him to call and he called on the fourth day. I didn't hear it ring, but still the telephone and answering machine told me I had missed it. I didn't bother checking for messages until 40 minutes before I had to go babysitting. Then, of course, I called back and he's not home. After berating myself for being so stupid, I proceeded to Karen's.

When he called back, Emily came to take over babysitting Robert and I went with Alistair to the movies. I felt so close to him. The urge was there, but again I felt restraint. I wanted to do something. I felt it. He knew I felt it. Did he feel it? There is something there. It just needs to be brought out. One first move is probably all it would take. He does something to me. I wore that sweater he liked.

"Does it cover hickies?" he asked.

"Yeah," I said "but it depends on where they are."

He turned to me "So what do you like to do? You don't play pool or video games, so what do you do? It's pick on Angela time."

All I could do was smile; I love it when he says my name. He clears my mind and slows down my brain in a good way. I love being with him.

After I got home he called. It was weird, being on the phone.

"Tell me something." he said.

I struggled, "The words are there, it just that they are not going to come out of my mouth." I said.

"So write me a letter." he responded.

I could easily write, because it's just paper that is listening to me. But on paper that will be going to him? We kept talking but my pen started its own voyage.

Dear Al: Why is my mind running around in circles because of you? We've gone out to two movies. The first I was uncomfortable being there with you. If you put your arm around me I would have put up with it, but not enjoyed it. I liked you but I didn't really know you.

I was really starting to like you, but there were many contradictions going on in my mind. There's the term "friends", the boundaries that existed and those that changed into something more. It seems as though our relationship sits on the borderline, swirling back and forth. This is what perplexes me most. I tell myself to let it go, let whatever happens happen. But it's not that easy when I'm thinking about it constantly and when I think about you to the extent that I do.

It seemed as though tonight I was comfortable enough with you to actually let these thoughts of physically being with you into my mind. But that wasn't the only thing I was thinking about...I was remembering and treasuring the first time we ever really talked, it was at Sue's sleigh ride party. Then semi-formal was another interesting night. We said we'd go "as friends", but still there is always something telling me that it was more. I really started to like you but kept telling myself that we were just friends. I don't regret telling you that I like you.

Right now I'm thinking of you and smiling to myself. If wishes came true, you would be beside me right now.

It's odd how strange these feelings are presently. I'd tell you right now how I feel if you called. It would have been nice to feel like this on Thursday before you picked me up. It'd be nice if I'm in a similar mood next time we are alone together. We've never really had good physical contact. The dances at semi were nice, with your arms wrapped around me, mine around you. The marina was interesting, holding hands. All small things and still comforting, any of which I'd enjoy right now. I'll see you in less than nine hours and by that time almost half of these persistent emotions will have subsided and the strength of them gone because of the lack of expression. Maybe with all these thoughts inside me I'll have a good dream. But I still don't know how you feel, except you like my hair, my voice and you enjoy talking to me. Then again I enjoy talking to you. I don't want it to end. Call me.

Angela

It was interesting the journal entries that followed that letter. None of them were about Alistair. Did I give it to him? Did he respond? I can't remember. I have to assume I didn't. Alistair started spending more time talking to this other girl; I spent a lot of time talking to Mike. As yearbook editor I had a lot of photographs to develop, and he worked at the store I frequented. *Mike brought me back to the crazy me I missed. The crazy me I was with Delia. It was amazing how easily we started talking. He was in the food court and I sat down and everything just progressed.*

Alistair made a comment that he can't see me in a relationship or only liking one guy. I think that pushed me into something with Mike. His words of encouragement were "At least it would be good with someone experienced."

It's April 13th. I went downtown for lunch today to see Mike. We were chatting about the weekend. He was being playful and used sign language so no one else saw him say "I want to have sex with you."

I signed back "ok." I want him to come over, but I fear once we start, I may not be able to stop. He is fun, light hearted and playful. A great friend but we would never be serious. The party at his place last weekend was good even with his fiancé there. We had been close before I found out about her. He has attempted since, but I've been hesitant.

At lunch he told me, "I'm going for an AIDS test."

What? I tried to slow myself down. "Wow that sounds like a scary test. How many people have you been with?"

There was no answer.

Maybe I was too judgmental in my wording. "Sorry, I shouldn't have asked." I said.

"It's always better to be safe and test." he responded.

The image of him coming over tonight was just squashed. Did he really just say that? We've gone out how many times, and he's telling me this now? My mind started spinning. I know we kept talking, but I couldn't think or listen to him anymore. I was at the library after lunch and Benji, an honest and blunt friend, showed up; he cleared my head and nicely reminded me of all that is morally correct. That's something only he or Alistair could do in a way I'd listen.

I called Alistair, but he is talking about looking for a place to get his new girlfriend alone. That call was not helpful. Now I'm feeling alone. Alistair is the only guy whom I believe I can fully trust and I am still attracted to him and his personality.

The next entry was undated. I'm not sure what changed. It's only been a week or so since he told me he was engaged, but tonight he told me the engagement was off. I had this reawakened sense of defiance mixed with falling for him. He came over and got physical really fast and I think I was in need of some physical attention. I enjoyed the contact, but it seemed weird. Almost like he was trying to make me feel sorry for him, and then get me to trust him. All sense of deviance is lost – it feels like we are now partaking in childish games. If the engagement is off, why can't we tell anyone what's going on? There weren't any firsts or anything, but he was the most enjoyable. I wonder how things would have gone if Alistair made a move like Mike did.

We were at a party at Sue's place when Mike decided he needed to tell me something. He told me that he's coming out of the closet. That's two of them now! Both were good friends turned boyfriends and came out of the closet after less than a month of us dating. Mike evidently is bisexual. He said he still likes me, and he likes girls, but he likes guys too. Guess I like the caring and attentive, but also open and adventurous guys? I don't know. I'm trying not to take it personally.

Later in university he became a strong advocate. Someone I knew at the same university was nice enough to forward me a copy of the article "Defining your Sexuality."

Today is, for some people, a day of special significance. Many of you will be unaware that today is what's known as Global Coming Out Day (GCOD). Today is the day when closeted gays, lesbians and bisexuals around the world are invited to take an axe to the proverbial closet door and hack it to irreparable bits. Or, if that's too big a step, at least to peek out through the keyhole....

June 1995. Alistair called last night. It saddens me to think that I will only see him for another two weeks. He's leaving for summer for army training and I won't get to see him at all. He was one of the reasons I wanted to stay in town. Why do I like him so much? It made me wonder, and I came to the conclusion that I trust him. There are very few people I let into my heart enough to trust. Emily is the only other one I can think of.

That's what was different…other boys were fleeting crushes. With Alistair it was a slow growing comfort. He was the first one who I really let get to know me. The first one I truly trusted. It seems as if this was the reason for my strong emotions towards him, and for my fear to act on them and change what we had.

I wrote him a letter and bought him a top-of-the-line Swiss Army knife, something he had talked about wanting for a long time.

I don't really know how to say the things I'm feeling presently.
You brought me through many a vicissitude that would have been
more difficult without you. You were the first male I have allowed
myself to trust. I wanted to thank you for the time you gave me.
The sound of your voice comforted me instantly when I was in
need of solace. You have calmed me many a time without knowing
and I thank you for this. Your friendship has meant a lot to me.
I wanted to do something for you but I didn't know what. Then
it hit me I may be gone before you get back, so I decided that I'd
have to say good bye now. I hate to leave you – thanks for being
there. I know I'll miss you.

Angela

I gave him the letter and the knife. He loved it. His girlfriend also got
him a Swiss Army knife, but it only had two tools. He told me she was upset
that I got him one that was so much better.

Alistair was back for just a week before I had to go. We went to the
movies and then to this cappuccino shop. We talked for hours. He was in
a spazzy mood; we went from happy to sad every few minutes. We talked
about the past year, his time in military training this summer, and how
the time apart was preparing us for the year ahead. I'm going to miss him
so much. I'll miss his voice, his piano playing... We've had plenty of long
talks before, but tonight was different. I wish he said 'see you later' but he
said "goodbye."

"Just one more hug." he said. I know it feels like goodbye, but the words
are so much harder to hear. I really enjoy being with him. I know I'm going
to miss him greatly. We sat on my porch trying to say goodbye for two
hours. Time's up; it's almost morning.

He left and I can't sleep. I'm leaving in a few hours. Our lives are
changing and I know we'll never go back to being what we were. What will
I miss most about him? I'll miss the adventures. He was a bit reckless and

always seemed to want to impress. One night we were out for a ride at the marina and he wanted to see how fast he could drive. He made it to his goal of 100km before he had to slam on the breaks and make a 90 degree turn to avoid the snow bank and lamp post. We made a bit of an impact, but it was gentle enough not to leave a mark. He took over the best friend role better than anyone else could have. I could sit and listen to him for hours. Music connected us; spirituality connected us. We spent many nights on the phone talking about God and why things happen the way they do. Judaism just made sense when he talked.

Time's up. As effortless tears gently roll down my face, I think of all I shall miss. My mom took me to the marina for my last time. The gentle waves, the ocean craves, the dreams of tomorrow I'll find. I feel the warmth of the sun on my back. I wonder about you, but what else can I do. I feel like I've run out of time. Everything is gone. Peace enters me, the waves rock me, and the smell of water clings to me. I could remain in this tranquillity forever. Still, reality is overpowering, and I open my eyes. I know I must go. I know I must be brave. A new world is before me.

I made a mixed tape to listen to on our drive. I put it in as we drove away. It started with Whitney Houston's song I Will Always Love You. "... Bittersweet memories that is all I'm taking with me. So, goodbye, please, don't cry..." My mom turned if off. We were both in tears. We drove the next hour in silence.

University Life 1995-2000

Journeying forward holding my head
high and terrified of the unknown

8

The Distance I Must Wander

y eyes fell on an alcohol label; I pictured the contents of the bottle and fondly remembered the friend I shared it with. Intense friendships developed quickly in residence. *Saturday, September 2nd, 1995, my first night in residence. I've met a few people, my roommate and others on the floor. Still, I wonder why I don't miss everyone. Perhaps it is because I feel like either I'm in a dream and when I wake up everyone will still be near, or perhaps it is that I feel like I've always been here and everything else is a dream. I miss Alistair but I know he's not that far away.*

I met Kate. We connected immediately. We went on our first frosh event, it was a pub crawl. With each new location it got better and better. At our last stop we stayed a bit longer. Kate and I made it on stage to dance. Some guy made eye contact with me and held it a few times. Later he pulled me over to talk with him. Weirdly, he had nice eyes at the beginning, but I don't know, after dancing with him a short while and drinking the Long Island iced tea he got me, he just turned scary. He freaked me out so Kate and I took off and walked home.

September 10th. I hope this is a mood swing, because I feel like crap. I don't feel as if I fit in and I'm not in the mood to try to. I enjoy sitting by myself, but I wish that someone was with me. Maybe I don't belong. Matt, if I had said "horribly" when you asked how I was, (man, I love your eyes) would I be here now, alone, talking to myself? I just want a hug. What if I focused on happy thoughts, like raindrops on roses? I feel like vomiting. I'm sick of my life. I'm sick of death and still I welcome it. Anything must be better than this world we inhabit.

The guys are next door. I should go and join in, say something to involve myself in the conversation. Even if I can't find anything to say, I can start a conversation with one or two people. I can talk to others around the girls, right? Of course I can, but I just feel so self-conscious around them. That's why I liked hanging out with the guys the first week. We talked so easily. It was playful with Matt especially. We chased each other with silly putty, had tickle fights, stole that guy's clothes from the washroom, I listened to him and his friend play the guitar, we put our names on the rival resident advisor's window. There are so many good feelings and memories already, but the girls just seem to want to chat about others, be judgmental, talk and not do things. I just don't connect with them.

So I went to talk. It's not me. I don't get along with them. Matt said, "Lose the attitude; it doesn't fit your personality." Yeah, he thinks he knows me so well. Is it attitude? I'm quiet because I feel out of place. He prefers the more relaxed me? Me too. Why does he have to have a girlfriend? It hasn't even been two weeks. God, I love the way he sees right through me.

September 21ˢᵗ. I met Dan while out at the Music Café and we've chatted a few times since. He wanted me to open up to him so he could learn the mystery behind my eyes. We went for a walk through the graveyard across the street, since it has great walking paths. Dan is a bit more into the Gothic scene than anyone I've really hung out with, so I figured he could handle the stories he was asking for. He is the one who chose the graveyard for our walk. He is the one who said he wanted to get to know me. So I told him.

I told him about my dad's murder. I started with "I had just gone to pick up my mittens for a skating party..."

"Wow, you've been through a lot." he told me.

I should have stopped there but didn't. I told him about my Grandma sitting up from her coma completely lucid, staring and pointing at me, telling me not to take any pictures as though she had heard my family's earlier conversation.

Dan seemed spooked. Maybe I went too deep too fast. We didn't even talk as we walked back. Why do guys want to know "the mystery behind the eyes" if they are not strong enough to be my man?

My life sucks, but Alistair's words still come to me: "It is only in the darkness we can see the stars." When things are good, we don't often seem to stop and appreciate them, but when things suck, you better understand what it is you want and it teaches us to accept the beauty when it does present. I miss Alistair so much!

Matt wanted to talk today, September 22ⁿᵈ, about his drunken stupor in my room on his birthday. He said, "Thank you for not taking advantage of the situation."

My response was honest. "It was hard not to."

He's such a philosopher. He told me, "A situation defined as real is real in its consequences."

Hold up! So he was in my room, we hung out and were drunk. How was the situation defined? What are the consequences? Should I have made a move, because it equates to having done something? How do you define our relationship? What do your actions say? You tempted me when you said "Call me back some day!" You tempted me when you kissed my hand. You tempted me when you look into my eyes a bit too long. You tempted me when we're watching TV and our eyes meet and hold contact during the romantic moments. Then, you hold my hand and shivers scamper thought my whole body. Tell me the consequence because I'd happily act! Oh, but you still have your girlfriend, right?

Oh my God, you know that guy whose clothes I stole... it turns out it was Joe. I was chatting with Joe today, September 26th, and he was talking about his first weeks here and that someone stole his clothes while he was in the shower and he had to run back to his room naked. I started laughing. He didn't think it was so funny. "That was you?" I asked.

"Yeah, why?" he said, not seeing the same humour.

"I was the one who stole them." I said. His expression changed from the hurt embarrassed look of being mocked when he was being open and honest about his experiences to a mischievous yet tough guy façade.

"Now I have to punish you." he said as he inched closer.

"Really?" I looked at him, smiling. "What are you going to do?"

"Strangle you. Do you trust me?" he asked.

"No." I responded. He was now standing inches from me.

"Close your eyes." he instructed, his tough guy approach getting softer.

Slowly I could feel his breath and then his warm lips on mine. Wow, he was an amazing kisser. I'm just sorry I missed getting to watch his naked body run back to his room.

I've been spending a lot of time with Joe, I just feel so comfortable with him. I kept the label from the bottle we worked through tonight. He's the first one I've really started telling the stories to. He can handle them. I feel like I can trust him with anything. Maybe the drink helped, and maybe his comforting touch helped. It just feels like there is a connection already there and I've known him forever.

October 5th. They announced the verdict in the OJ Simpson trial. Everyone was in the lounge watching: not guilty. Shivers ran up and down my whole body. Joe's eyes met mine. I thought I was going to lose it. I was sitting in the court room all over again. He knew I needed out, no words necessary. He stood up, took me by the hand and walked me back to my room. He knows me better than anyone I've ever known. What if the verdict in my dad's trial was not guilty? I hate life. I hate violence. I was so past gone. Joe sat there and held me.

In November, Joe and I got in a fight. I started dating Steve and Joe started dating someone else too. She feels he's not true to her, that he's hung up on me. She tried killing herself! She was with the resident advisor when Joe came to get me. He wants me to lie to her and tell her that nothing is happening between us. But I ran back to him after Steve tried kissing me and ended up licking my face; Joe is such a better kisser. Is anything happening between us? If yes, why aren't we together? Why is he even with her? I went to see her. She was in tears…so I told her what she needed to hear. She had seen Steve and the flowers he brought me. (Of course she didn't know about that horrible kiss.) I told her I was dating him, and there was nothing going on with me and Joe. Is it ok to lie in life or death situations? Is it really my fault? His fault? What about her fault? Life is messed up.

I found an unopened letter post marked November, 1995. I had written to myself:

Dear Angela: I know you must be doing pretty horrible right about now, but I want you to know that you've survived a lot and I'm really proud of you. I don't know anyone else who could have put up with everything you have and you did a great job. Look at all your achievements. You survived so much more than what should be expected of any person. I am so proud of you. You are the number one person in my life and you deserve love. Don't ever think that you don't deserve the best. Nobody will ever be any better to you than you. You've had some good times in your life. It wasn't all heartache and tragedy. You loved scuba diving.

Alistair made you feel so special before you left for university, "Just one more hug." Remember Kevan and the box of chocolates he gave you at school on Valentine's Day. Just remember that I will always be there and that people do care about you. Think happy thoughts. When you really want love, you'll find it waiting for you!

Angela.

Mark, one of the guys from fifth floor that I've chatted with a few times, came down to the fourth floor lounge tonight while I was studying. I had lost a bet with Matt about how many beers it would take to get Mark drunk as the three of us were hanging out in my room. Clearly for Mark it was just one, but Matt and I needed and enjoyed significantly more. I love drinking with Matt! I love being with Matt. Anyway, Mark has tried hitting on me a few times, and keeps telling me no one understands him like I do. I talk to him, but I've told him flat out I'm not interested. Tonight he was drunk and rude, and went too far. He came up to give me a hug but was all hands and completely out of line. I pushed him back and smacked him when he grabbed me and got in my face trying to kiss me. Matt's girlfriend was visiting and walked into the lounge and rescued me. We went back to Matt's room.

"Mark was all over her and she was trying to push him off." his girlfriend told him.

"Are you ok?" he asked as he hugged me.

He turned to his girlfriend, still holding me and said "She is one of the few cool people from fourth floor." As he let the hug end and separate he asked "Where's Mark?"

"He's still in the lounge." she told him.

He went and pounced on Mark and threw a couple of really good punches at him. The funny thing was Matt's response; it was almost as if we were dating. Am I allowed to love Matt when his girlfriend is the one who rescued me? I feel so guilty liking a guy with such a nice girlfriend.

'Thank you' just seemed insufficient, so I said it as I stole a second hug. It was so nice to feel his arms around me, but as I breathed in the moment, imprinting the memory, I couldn't help but see his girlfriend, standing only a few feet away. There are a few amazing guys out there...often taken...

December 1995. Yeah, so...stages have passed. Platforms have been achieved, and all else left in a blur. I'm left here with no direction, wondering where I stand and what I should do. Our friendship is deeper than any I've ever known. But if we start dating, his ex might try to kill herself again.

"Are you going?" Joe asked.

"Yes." I told him.

"I'm sorry." he said.

"Don't be." I responded.

The self-talk started inside my head. I can't make a big deal about it: if I did, I'd lose him. He is my best friend and more, and the only one who knows all of my stories. If I expected anything beyond being friends, I'd be an emotional wreck if it wasn't reciprocated. I wandered aimlessly, unsure of who I was and what I had done. "But most of all I'm scared I might walk out of this room and never feel for the rest of my whole life, the way I feel when I'm with you." The words from Dirty Dancing best explained my thoughts. I went home for the holidays and got a card in the mail from Joe. "No matter the season or the reason." it said. I loved it.

I had a nasty horrible dream. Please God, tell me there was no truth to that dream, and even still I know I won't believe you. Was I that little girl? God help me. Sex changes everything. Use a lending hand and keep me sane. Sometimes it feels so good to cry. The loneliness grows over. The curtains close. I've been left on a dark empty stage with nothing, naked to all around me, vulnerable to all who care, if there is anyone. The curtains open. The spotlight is on me and I tell my story. I was sexually abused as a young child. The light has consumed my eyes. I'm blind to anyone or anything. I stare at it and cry.

The monthly schedule has been disrupted. What should have come yesterday has not. It's starting to scare me. Thoughts of having a baby with Joe enter my mind. I see us together as we watch, our little girl running in a large open field filled with wildflowers. I don't know if that is from a previous lifetime or a future still to come. I know nothing has been created within me this time. It's just one of those feelings. My mind needs to worry, or focus on something… but what if? I'm not ready for this. The Cabala says that God counts the tears of women. I think they just understand the world better. Thanks for the call and words of wisdom, Alistair. I think you understand me better. God grant me the courage to change the things I can.

Chains of Love

These feelings that I'm feeling make me feel so fine,
I slowly sip my wine, getting drunk by nine.
I can't hold back because I'm lost in love,
Head stuck in clouds above and I'm dying.
Because I love you, but I can't have you,
And still I want you, but I can't find you,
And I need you so… baby.
These feelings that I'm feeling make me feel so fine,
I slowly sip my wine, getting drunk by nine.
I can't hold back because I'm lost in love,
Head stuck in clouds above and I'm dying.
So baby come to me and honey rescue me,
And hold me tight for all eternity.
Then I'll be free, from these chains of love.
Yeah honey I'll be free, from these chains of love.
Angela, 1995

So it came, late, but it came. I don't know what I'm doing anymore. I'm back at school but I need to be alone. I'm totally sick of people, yet I long to be held. I want to just run back upstairs. Joe always makes things seem better. I can go from mania to depression in a matter of minutes. This is not good. I'm on the verge of renting a hotel room and just hiding out for a day. That might be healthier. I hate not having anywhere to retreat to. I feel like I'm running, but I'm so scared. I had that dream again. I hate this. My throat is dry and I can't breathe. I'm almost 20 years old and I'm frightened by crazy nightmares of my childhood. It was so vivid, so real, and I couldn't get away. Where is the person who can drag me out of this? Joe's ex was threatening suicide again. He is back with her, and we are back to "friends." I need help.

Reading week 1996. Joe and I were just starting to talk again. I wanted to go visit him, but I knew if I did that I'd want to stay. I really missed him. I distracted myself, studied, looked at houses for next year and watched movies. Today he gave me a huge guilt trip for my actions. I had to do it to stay sane, but it hurt him and I was sorry for his pain.

Today is March 9th, Joe's birthday. I didn't think he cared. He kept going back to his girlfriend. Well, he set me straight. I did mean a lot to him, he told me. He was just getting back at her, getting her devoted to dump her, crush her, ruin her. Well, he smelled so good, I didn't want to leave his room. We were meeting up with her and a few others at the pub. Walking there together, starting off with his arm around me, distancing ourselves as we approached and letting go of his hand when we got to the bar, letting him walk in first without me, keeping it secret: it's all too hard. I am in the shadows, overpowered by whatever is happening with his girlfriend. Why am I not enough? If he cared about me as much as he said he does, and his intent with her is as he says it is, then I shouldn't have to sit in the shadows. As much as I love him and know we have an intese connection, I have to let him go and just wait until they are finished.

After the early days with Matt with emotions running high, Mark continued to talk to me and slowly became tolerable, but I wasn't expecting this. Mark proposed to me. He was on the top balcony and talking to me then walked down the stairs. Said he can't imagine being without me and asked if I'd consider marrying him so we can stay together. He offered me a ring. It was the right level of intensity but the wrong guy. What good are material keepsakes if there are no emotions tied to them?

I'm living with Liz next year. She was my neighbour and always there to assist with decisions, especially pertaining to fifth floor boys, even if she had to tackle me to the ground to reinforce her opinion. I suppose I was always able to make the final decision. She was there when I needed her, and I was happy to do anything for her.

I'm going to miss her so much over the summer. I don't know what I would do without her. She knows when to come over. She knows what to do. I know things don't get better with a wave of a wand but I feel better with her near. The situation still exists, but I feel as though with her, I can struggle through it all. She'll always love me and help me out when she can. I love her so much. It makes things easier knowing I'm not fighting through all this crap alone anymore. I could hardly watch her leave, even though I'll be living with her next year. I'll just have to survive four months without the comfort of having her next door.

I can't believe it's over, that first year is almost done. A friend from fourth floor and I got each other journals for our birthdays and we had everyone sign them and put in a picture of themselves. Some entries were so detailed:

> Well, it has been a great year. I still remember the day I met you. It was the Sunday of Labour Day weekend, September 3rd. Wow. A lot has happened since then: lots of tears, laughs and dilemmas! It has been great talking to you about all of our problems we always seem to find some sort of answer. It has been great that we can talk about our fathers. I believe that is what has made us such good friends, along with the other things we have done this year. Just remember I created the name "Hoover!" Boy, what a night. I have never been forcefully put into an inverted tuck before. It was a rather

interesting situation. Well we can both say that we have definitely met a lot of different people while we were here. So how's Daniel, Farouk, Matt, Steve, Bill, Mark, etc... and oh yes Joe.

You are the best. Our lives are never dull here, let me tell you. Just remember, don't watch any scary movies without me. I'm always going to be there for you. We can write to each other, and I'm sure we can visit over the summer.

Well, I have slowly lost my words. I don't want to get too mushy because I don't want to cry. Let me tell you, though, I will definitely miss you this summer. I will always remembember our very late night walks along the river front, and our roller blade trips. I will guarantee that I will be able to make it down any sort of hill without screaming next September. I make a promise of that. I wish you nothing but the best, for you deserve all the happiness in the world. We have experienced enough sadness at such a younge age to last a lifetime. It can't get any worse. If it does we will help eachother through it. I promise. You have been a great friend and you'll always be a great friend to me. You may be leaving me for the summer but you will never be forgotten. All of my love and best wishes, your friend always.

Kate.

Other entries I can hardly place, one made me reflect:

Well, we had some good times and we had some bad times, but we had them together and that's what really matters. You better never forget me and if you are reading this... and you can't place exactly where I fit into your life, just white out this page. I never want to be just a faint memory in your mind. Later, sweetie.

Mark.

It took me a moment to remember there were two Marks on the floor. I hardly recognized the guy.

How many people from residence would play a lasting role in my life? How many of them could I remember now, over 15 years later? My strongest memories are of my core group (Liz, Kate, Becky, Joe, Mike, and Orville) and a few random friends like Matt who seemed to come and go, still leaving quite an impact. So many other friends who seemed critical at that time were more challenging to remember even with the journal entries. One boy, Farouk I had completely forgotten about until I read Kate's comments, so I searched for a journal entry to find out who he was. Evidently he was some boy who I met one night when I was trying to get Joe out of my mind. He came really close to being a one night stand, but I called it off before things got too intense.

My birthday came along and the residence was almost empty. Joe and I were supposed to go out together, but didn't. He was already wasted when I got back from the show. He said a lot of nice stuff. I said thank you, then asked why he waited until he was drunk to say it. We got into another fight. I ended it saying "I love you, and I can say it sober." I kissed him and continued, "Go on with your life. Get back to me when you can talk without alcohol." He ended up going out with his friends, I went out with mine, and I'm leaving in a few days.

Nyles was eager to be the first to take me out, asking when I'd be coming home. Wasn't he the one who said he didn't want me thinking about him years later, that it was over and we needed to move on? We went out Sunday, April 28th, the day after I got home. We went for dinner and then to the lake. It was beautiful, with a light fog rolling in. We sat at a picnic table watching the water. I missed the nature and wilderness most when I was away. We sat and talked for a while, and then he got up and got down on one knee. Oh, no, I thought. What is he doing? Was that a ring box he just pulled out? "We never should have broken up. I was lucky to have you and will never find anyone as good as you. Will you marry me?"

Had he really just done that? I had a hard time not laughing. He should have thought about that before our messy break up just a few months after my dad was murdered! I think I may have laughed out loud. "Nyles, I am not the person I was, and neither are you. It would never work."

He called the next day apologizing for kissing me and said he felt like he had been pushing himself on me. "It's just that I really like you. I'm sure you know that by now and it's obvious that you don't think of me in the same way. I meant it when I asked you to marry me. Your friendship really means a lot to me. I don't want to lose it."

Perhaps they were good boosts to my ego, first Mark's proposal then from Nyles. What a month. Yet I know neither boy is right for me, and the one I do want is nowhere near ready for commitment. I think the best part of the whole proposal was telling Alistair and the extent of his surprise. I missed Alistair – he's one of the reasons I'm happy to be back.

9

Chocolate Makes it Better

My chocolate fortunes were folded up hiding under the bottom panel. They were my comfort and solace after the worst fight ever. They remind me I have little control over opposing agendas. Sometimes all I have is a box of chocolates.

It's was good to be back at University. I've never been so happy for it to be September! But I had these stabbing pains in my head, and the doctors sending me for tests, to rule out a tumour. I called Joe – the pain isn't stopping. He said he'd come with me to the clinic if I wanted. I went without him, comforted by his offer. Today as I was leaving, he was there. So we talked, and I felt better. A horrible day turned perfect. It's just like there is a bigger picture and I will be taken care of, like everything will be ok. Maybe all those things we talked about over the summer will materialize.

I love going out to the clubs. There's just something about the energy! Out here, my name is Michelle. The music is so loud it penetrates every molecule of my body. Tonight Kate and I went out to the pub; she's one of my favourite dancing buddies. Amanda, my new housemate, also happened to show up. It was an amazing night! I get such a rush from dancing with them both. Kate was buying pitchers of lime and vodka (it was the anniversary of her dad's death). It tasted like sweet lemonade going down. How much is too much? Mike and the boys from residence showed up; they always take such great care of us that Kate and I had a third pitcher. It's funny how we judge our level of acceptable inebriation based on the boys who will walk us home. Mike is tall and strong guy who is full of attitude and still sensitive and caring. He was seemingly always there when I needed him. We danced until last call. Never has a hot dog from a vendor tasted so good!

The reunion was great and put me in a state of reflection, bringing back memories of stories, secrets and the journeys of friendships that made it anywhere near my walls. Phrases came to mind including:

"I could have… but didn't."

"A situation defined as real, is real in its consequences."

"Lose the attitude; it doesn't fit your personality."

"I love you; go on with your life."

"Am I not enough?"

"Never underestimate the power of estrogen."

"What good are games if nobody wins?"

Each phrase matched with an event ranging from play, to love, to breakups and tears, all treasured moments in time.

I found an unopened letter post marked September 3rd, 1996. The journal entry from that day poorly introduced it: *What just happened?!?!? I have no one left to trust, no one left to talk to, so I wrote myself a letter and mailed it, which is the only way to get it all out and still keep it private:*

> *Well that was the biggest and most emotional fight I've ever had. Never have I felt as alone and empty as I do right now. I know my sister Emily would be there for me, but I don't want any listening ears or wandering eyes to have their chance. Liz and I aren't talking anymore. Last year I told Liz about what happened at Christmas. She thought it was a mistake, but seemingly accepted it once I told her how much I liked him.*
>
> *Liz told me "Joe's ex-girlfriend came up to me at the reunion and asked about you and Joe. She asked if he had been over, if he and you had sex, if he and you are going out. I played dumb and told her I'm only her roommate, I don't monitor her every move. I don't know what they are doing."*
>
> *Kate is upset. She said "Joe is being such a jerk to his ex." She continued, "Joe and his ex have been together recently; do you know he's playing you?" Anyway, Kate is not talking to me anymore. Joe was the last man standing and the only unknown. I needed to figure out what was going on. I needed the truth.*
>
> *So Joe came over and we had a really intense conversation. "I still like you a lot, but I have to back off because of all the stuff I'm hearing." I told him.*
>
> *He blamed me, saying "You told Kate and Orville that we are having sex. Liz told my ex that you and I are having sex and Liz had to leave the pub because you were crying about me and ruined her birthday!"*
>
> *"What? I was out with Mike and Bill having fun, not crying! I told Liz and Emily about you and I but that was last year!" I was getting angry.*

I had to breathe. "I'm sorry for whatever my friends may have said." I told him.

"Tell anybody who says anything about me to say it to my face." he said.

"I will." I told him.

He then crushed me, "I'm going to deny our having sex, if anyone asks."

"Ok." I said wanting to crawl into a hole and disappear.

"I trusted you. I told you things I would have never told anyone. I came to see you when I was upset or down, because being around you put me in a better mood and now this happens. What was going through your mind?" he asked me. "That's all I want to know. Friends don't do things like this to each other."

I was ready to die. He doesn't believe me. He thinks I'm guilty. "I'm sorry; I told you everything I know. What else can I say?"

"Don't say things you don't mean." he responded.

With that I flipped. "You don't believe that I'm sorry? You are the last person in the world that I would want to hurt." I stared into his eyes; feelings of remorse for having spoken consumed me. "If I could go back and never say anything to Liz or Emily, I would, but I can't. Last year I told Liz, trusting her, and now I'm trying to explain myself to you for her actions. If you don't understand how much you mean to me there is no point of me even trying! I would never want you mad at me." I said.

"Oh, I'm not mad, just disappointed!" he responded.

Why not just kill me now? I thought to myself, biting my tongue to stay silent.

His tone changed with my silence, "So why would Liz and Kate do that to you?" he asked.

"I don't know, maybe because they know how much I like you and they don't like you, so they are trying to separate us. Clearly it's working. You are 'disappointed' with me. They tell you stories *and blame me for it. Then they tell me different stories that also vary from the truth. So I get annoyed with you, tell you I have to back off and they continue shooting you down. You are told stories and you get to the point of blowing up and put me at fault so you don't talk to me. So maybe they had a plan and maybe they've succeeded."*

His voice softened. "No they didn't, and they won't." He paused, and then continued… "It will take a long time to come even close to where we were."

My head hurts. I'll never know if believing in hope can let him see that what I said was true. I haven't lied to him. Right now I don't care if he believes me or not. He's got too much sorting out to do on his own. I can only hope that he knows I'm sorry for whatever I did, I'm sorry for the things he believes that are not true, and most of all, I'm sorry that he has to go through all of this.

It's been 45 minutes since he walked away. God, I miss him so much. It kills me because I didn't say any of that and he doesn't believe me. So I'm left with nothing. No Joe, no Liz, no Kate. I have no one to talk to, no one to trust. My best friendships were all destroyed tonight. I ended up with a box of chocolates and kept two of the fortunes. The first said: "When I saw you, I fell in love, and you smiled because you knew." The second one was: "As rare as true love is, it is not as rare as true friendship."

November 1996. Almost two months later, he sent me a brief email.

> *When all is done and well,*
> *The patient still thrives.*
> *First fruits are cherished,*
> *And the wise shall rule.*
>   *Peace.*

My response:

> *You bring sad smiles to my face.*
> *Sadness, because I miss you so much.*
> *Joy, because you're still thinking of me*
> *And peace…because one day, we'll be ok.*

10

Loving Clubs and Drinking

*I*t was Friday the 13th of September 1996; I went to karaoke night at the pub with Amanda, my new roommate. I love singing. I love that I got into the choir at university and get to perform. I'm glad my mom made us sing so much that I feel somewhat confident in my abilities. Tonight I got my power from the DJ. I started singing in a high soprano and she told me to drop my key, that I couldn't do it. After I did, she said it was beautiful and suggested we do a duet next time.

I was out at the Music Café. This guy came up next to me told me "I like your combat boots."

"Thanks, I got them in Sea Cadets." *I told him. He started dancing with me.*

"Can I get you a drink?" *he offered.*

"Thanks, I'd love a Long Island iced tea." *We went up to the bar together. (I never accepted a drink I didn't get from the bar tender. There were too many stories of friends who had something else added.) We danced another song or two.*

My friends were leaving so I told him "I have to go."

He looked shocked. "I bought you a drink; what do I get for it?" *he asked.*

I looked back at him and smiled. "You got a thank you, a dance and smile from a girl who's going home with her friends." *He smiled and shook his head as I walked away.*

As much as I loved the clubs, the dancing and walking on desolate streets afterwards, it was the conversations with friends that occurred in those states that I loved most. Throughout conversations with friends I learned that I was not alone in the abuse I had experienced. *Tonight a good friend was having a rough time. I was listening and attempting to comfort her. I reached to brush away a tear when she leaned in and kissed me. There was no way I was going to show any level of rejection. She needed to know I fully accepted her for who she was and I did.* Following that night, we went out to the bars a number of times. We also kissed (to arouse the guys) on more than one occasion. Together she and I could get any guy we wanted. The beer cap was from one of our nights out together.

Sometimes I wonder about friendships. Why we like who we like, what defines a friendship and what makes a relationship 'more than friends?' Another good friend recently suggested we give up men completely. As comfortable I was with her and as much as I thought at that time that it was a great idea, I knew it wouldn't work long term. Many girls I know keep too many things bottled up, secrets hidden; I think that's why I tend to trust guys and get along with them better.

I learned I am not the only one with a shell of walls surrounding me like a castle. My shell has 14 layers. A soul mate connection is at the core; pure love is obtainable although few reach this level, to get here there are many tests that must be passed. My walls are there to protect me, keep me safe and approach any new friendship with caution as well as an open mind.

I look at my walls as staircases one must climb to get over the wall and closer to me. The first wall is that of trust, and there only two platforms that must be reached. The first platform is the test of tolerance, sarcasm and pushing away as I determine what they can handle. If someone wants in, they need to be able to push through the crap and engage in meaningful interactions. The second platform is communication and willingness to share their stories. People who want to get to know me need to be able to talk and listen about superficial stuff and conversations that require some thought process. Anyone who knows me knows there are times I need both.

The second wall is that of games. The first platform in the staircase up the wall involves a series of intense stories to test their responses, empathy, trust and secrets. Starting with simple stories and simple secrets I can evaluate their response. How would they handle the deeper darker stuff? Do they reciprocate with stories of their own? Do they tell my stories? Do they come back?

The second platform is for those that do come back... Next is an evaluation of body language; analyzing their comfort levels as well as mine. So often I've said "Don't touch me!" My physical responses as well as theirs keep me in tune with the degree of safety I feel with their proximity. Lastly there is a series of questions to figure out who they are and if they are worthy of climb up the final wall. I want to know what they love most, what they fear most, what they are most proud of and most ashamed of. If basic trust is reciprocated these stories and questions should be easy. I need to know if they will hurt me, if they can handle all of me, the raw me. It is these answers that tell me most about anyone and allow for them to meet me in my most vulnerable enclosure.

The third wall is the most powerful and the longest climb. The first platform is the test of time, consistency and availability. Will they be there when I need them? Is their response consistent, can I depend on them? If they are there consistently when I need them they will get all the stories and I will be there for them and all of their stories.

The second platform of the third wall is total truth, honesty and reciprocation. In this last year, many have attempted and a few have succeeded in really getting to know me. Only three have made it to total truth, their stories and mine, reciprocated and trusted in another person. People who have touched my heart and I will always love. These are people who have seen me in my raw state and I theirs. Perhaps "loving the clubs" is about allowing ourselves to be in a relaxed state and feeling safe with someone we really care about.

The final platform is total trust, vulnerability and pure love, only one of the three continued the journey and I'm not sure I can tell the difference between that last platform and my core. I believe he is my soul mate. I know I can be vulnerable yet completely comfortable with him, knowing we both know the other as well as well as we know ourselves and perhaps better sometimes.

As I reflect years later, I wonder how these walls have changed… I feel transparency is so much easier than sarcasm and games. My stories are no longer as intense as they once seemed. A person's ability to listen and the depth of the conversations is still important. What I treasure is an open mind and comfort levels with complex issues and discussions. Time, truth, honesty also continue to be critical factors, but I've learned judgment, choice and spirituality play important roles in developing connections. I enjoy complex thinkers who challenge me to question why I think what I do and either confirm or explore further potentials. I use spirituality in the sense of being aware to the world and consciousness. So many people in my life exist in simple superficial relationships and very few move towards a meaningful and reciprocated connection. There continues to be just a select few that sit within my circle of people I feel connected to, perhaps that is one of the few things that does remain constant.

11

The Perfect Date

M y eyes then landed on that dime, stuck in the beer cap and covered by Joe's liquor label. Stuck between two amazing friends and adventures was Sam. This dime only reflects this one perfect night, not our whole time together. I actually don't remember the first time I met Sam. I fully believed he was the guy who came up to me at the Music Café and said he liked my combat boots. Months later, the guy who really did that commented on them again, validating Sam and leaving me without a memory of meeting Sam. At some point, however, we met and started talking in the quiet study room at the Students' Centre. He mentioned seeing me at the Music Café and I assumed he was the boots guy.

On September 22ⁿᵈ, 1996 we had our first date. What an amazing night! Sitting next to him in the theatre was great. We made random eye contact and held hands. Everything was so familiar, comfortable and perfect. We then went dancing at the Music Café, and being there next to him, pulled in close, moving as he moved, was perfect. Then we went for a walk along riverside, holding hands in the fresh night air. When we got back to his car he gave me a rose and sang the Fugees version of Killing Me Softly. His voice was beautiful, as if he was caressing each word. We kissed. His lips were soft, warm and full of passion. Sam is so beautiful.

We went back to my place and were talking on the sofa. I needed to know more about what he was like. After an amazing night, I just needed to know about what makes him who he is. Trying to get some info I asked him to "tell me something about what makes you, you."

"I've only been with one person before." he said, staring deep into my eyes. We were sitting snuggled close with limbs intertwined. "I'm planning to go to med school." The breath from his words was on my face, his mouth almost on mine now, "My biggest fear is losing you." He gave me a soft kiss. "And I'll never forget your eyes." He stayed until almost two in the morning.

He happened to forget his wallet, which seemed like a free offer to learn more about him and the perfect thing to leave to make sure we meet up tomorrow. Of course I had to open it. It was nicely organized: he had his identification, his bank card, some cash and a condom that didn't expire for another few months (at least I can assume he was being cautious and optimistic). I traded one of my dimes for one from his wallet to keep as a reminder of this perfect night. I called him to let him know he left it and he said he'd stop by tomorrow morning.

12

Lost Innocence

November 21st 1996. It's been two months… Tonight Sam and I had sex. The condom broke, it was such a mistake. I wasn't ready for it. The memories of a long forgotten assault arose and ruined everything. I was sucked away to memories of my childhood. Life was innocent once right? I stared at my baby picture. Would he have accepted my past experiences? Could I have told him? He is the first guy I liked, got and still liked a month later, even now, two months later. But I woke up this morning thinking of Joe, the only one who knows all my stories. Joe, I love you. Not because

we were intimate but because you never judged me, because you were my friend and because you had earned something very few people have; my trust, my total trust. You were the only one I found so far worthy enough, loved enough and trusted enough for me to expose my vulnerabilities to. I loved you. I made a conscious decision, a sober decision. I wanted you to be my first. I just had to wait until the right time. When it came, I wanted more, to be near you again, to let you know how much you mean to me.

I wanted you, but I wanted you to want me and only me. This was an impossible want. I felt I was always going to be the other girl in your eyes. I didn't care if you were with your girlfriend, or that other girl. We started as friends and it grew. You always made me feel special. Even when you irritated me, I was only frustrated because I knew I'd never have you to myself and it was the one thing I wanted more than anything. If only once you could have told me you wanted me and only me, you would have had me. Instead you started coming to me when you had time and it just didn't seem like enough anymore. I had to stop thinking about you. I deserved better.

I didn't want to be the other girl and I couldn't handle just being friends. So I focused on other guys and suddenly you had time for me. But I'm not with you, I'm with Sam and terrified to open up and try to trust someone else with all those stories that rule my life.

There are so many thoughts running through my head. I saw it, relived it, clear as yesterday. I need to talk to someone. It's dark. I lay there small and naked. Five years old. I wore a dress, he took it off. I don't sense him as being mad. But I am terrified. He holds onto my shoulders as I'm lying on the bed. He's at the side so as he pushes he holds me in place. Joe I need you.

I had to go talk to Joe. He's the only one who knows. He and I have been in rough shape since September, but I showed up on his door step and he let me in and listened. "Don't think" he said and he just held me close. I was safe.

December 4th I started seeing a new therapist and what a day I was given. I started it off with some Ativan. I went to the Computer Centre saw

Joe, started feeling drugs kicking in. Anti-anxiety drugs rock! I went to the Students' Centre and tried to study. I couldn't focus, I left, ran into Sal (a friend), we went for coffee and ended up at the Students' Centre again. We then went to the library and studied a bit, I saw Sam while I was leaving to look at my Law & Studies exam grade. It's so over between us. I'm not ready to tell him my stories and I can't be with him right now. So I went back to the Computer Centre and responded to an email from Joe '10 last things a woman would say' with the ones I'd happily say, he was still there, so we met up.

Joe came over and we studied until two in the morning. He told me those words I'd longed to hear for so long "I was prepared to drop everyone else for a serious relationship with you back in September and my feelings still haven't changed."

It has been two weeks since the flashback with Sam. Two weeks since the condom broke. Two weeks and he hasn't called. Two weeks of hormone changes, the morning after pills, waiting and testing. Joe was the one who was there giving me comfort. I asked him, "If I have to go get an abortion, would you come with me?"

He hugged me and said "You wouldn't have to ask." We started watching a movie and then he leaned over and kissed me... Sam and I are done, right?

Sam called, when I got back from Christmas Break. "I need to apologize for the last month. Can I see you?" Can he do that? Apologize for a whole month?

"Sure come over." I said.

It was almost three in the morning when he arrived. Seeing him was different than I had expected. After he said "Hello stranger" and gave a big hug, he said "I've been a real jerk lately haven't I?"

We went up to my room; I was freezing and crawled back under my big comforter. "So why have you been such a jerk lately?" I probed.

"When you were here all I wanted was to stay away, and then when you went home for the holidays, I missed you so much. I was scared. I had never been in that situation and I didn't know how to handle it. I have a friend who had a child and I saw how it impacted her life. I'm sorry. I didn't know how to deal with it. I just needed time to figure out my thoughts." he said seemingly trying to justify his actions.

It was a good attempt, I had to give him credit for that, but he already told me he was scared and I knew he ran. I guess I was kind of rude in that aspect, but I deserved more than that.

"How was it for you?" he asked.

"It really bothered me that you didn't call. It added to the confusion. I had to take the morning after pills, had crazy hormone imbalances and your avoidance made me question not only the event but if you even really cared for me. Do I mean anything to you? What kind of a relationship is this if any at all?" Verbal diarrhoea poured from my mouth.

My head and heart were in different places. My body aching for his touch, but I was so upset with him.

He asked "Can you forgive me?"

"Yes" I said, "but not for the right reasons."

"What are the right reasons?" he inquired.

"I don't know; I'm just having a hard time telling you something." I said, one more look into his eyes and I thought I'd collapse. "Remember the friend I told you about? We had got into a big fight?"

"Yeah." my words seemed to stop him and hijack the agenda.

"Well, we made up. I guess that's why it bothered me so much when you said what you did to Sal (Sal was a friend, no intimacy. Sal told me "Sam asked me 'Are you and Angela good friends?' I said 'No just friends.' Then Sam said 'Are you in it just to get some ass?' and then he walked away.") It wasn't Sal. It was someone else." The silence was deafening. He looked really upset, "I've been with him for the last month." I finished.

He didn't get angry though. He simply asked, "Do you still care for me?"

"I care about you a lot." I responded.

"That's all I need to know." he said as he hugged me, we kissed and then

I initiated, his body was so warm and soft. It felt so good. Fully satisfied and laying in his arms we promised each other we would tell each other how we were feeling and prevent anything like this from happening again.

January 2nd I woke up feeling unsettled. When Sam is in my arms everything feels good, but there is still so much that needs to be said. It's just physical. He doesn't know me. I want to tell him what happened the first time we had sex. I want him to know about my past. Why can't I trust him? He knows nothing about me. I don't even know how to start.

You said you'd call January 7th and you haven't. If you need space take it, but don't tell me you'll call and leave me anticipating. I need to talk, I want to see you, but there is no follow through. I love you, it just doesn't seem reciprocated. I don't know how much longer I can hold out. I can't find you at school, you don't return calls. I have faith that if you really care you'll come back, but that doesn't mean I'm going to close myself off from the world.

The last 24 hours have been diverse. I got back from the criminology clubs' trip to Alcatraz January 14th and been crying for almost a week. I have the anti-anxiety medication still. I'm not sure if I would, but I am ready to. How many would it take? I'm sick of hurting. I had enough to drink with Liz; I came up to my room, sad and drunk, and saw my bible. I picked it up, the last two tear drops fell on to it and my headache ended. The pain ended too. I felt the new life enter me. I'm not sure as of now how much it has changed me, but the peace is one I haven't known for ages.

I met this new guy Eric at the Music Café and we connected immediately he grew up in Kalamazoo, I started calling him Kzoo. He is the quarter back for his university's football team. We talked for over an hour tonight, January 26th but it's weird. I feel connected to him. He oddly seems to have been able to acquire my trust quickly.

"You are a hard one to crack." he said.

"You are doing a good job." I responded.

There is a reason we met. He has all those characters of my best friends. He is as attractive as Sam, he probes my mind makes me think like Sal and

I feel as if I can trust him like Joe. If he lived next door it would be easy, but he lives in another city.

During the conversation he commented, "To get what you want, you are going about it the wrong way." I don't know how he knows what to say and when but he's absolutely right.

Kzoo was the guy I needed. Today (January 28th) Kzoo worked me through a discussion about my dad. We talked about religion, spirituality and purpose. By 2:30 this morning, I said "I forgive my dad." Kzoo gives me strength, feel so energized when I talk to him.

Am I completely crazy for following my heart? I feel happy. God makes things fall into place. I see love around me and that's what I want. He wants to be with me, convinced me that I'm loveable and that not all guys are alike. Do I love him? Not yet, I've known him less than a week, today is the 30th. Just thinking about him and the possibilities makes me smile though.

He just left. It's February 2nd and I miss him so much already. He was with me all weekend. This boy is amazing. He knows when something is bothering me, and all he wants to know is what it is. It felt good to be in his arms, against his body. I loved spending the night with him talking all night and innocently sleeping at his side. He's not trying to go physical saying he doesn't want to have sex until his wedding night. I told him a lot more than I intended to, but as hard as it was, I'm glad he reacted the way he did. He was great with my stories, encouraging me to continue telling him. Maybe that's what I have to do. Figure it out. I came so close to tears and I shouldn't have let him bring me so close. He knew and held me. The other thing that was really cute was when I awoke during the night, so did he and he said he couldn't go to sleep because I wasn't. I'm falling fast. When I awoke he was looking at me smiling.

"Wow," he said, "you are so beautiful." I loved waking up to him!

Wow…. February 3rd Kzoo asked a big question I'm not ready for. Could I do that? Contemplate marriage with this guy. His testosterone is too high. I don't know him well enough. Would he be physically abusive to kids? There was that time he said "I'm going to kick your ass." He was joking sure, but is it a red flag? What about those negative comments he said about that girl? Having dinner with his parents was insightful, but it was only one time. How is he to his mom? They said some strange stories during dinner. I don't know.

There is too much to lose. The communication is a new thing for me; it's a lot easier to tell him things than anyone else. I feel safe in his arms. I love the way he reacts to my stories. He gives me strength and courage to do things I normally procrastinate with. He helps ease my pain with words I need to hear. The rest of my life is so long, I don't want to make plans if I don't know I can keep them. Girlfriend status I could handle. Is he someone with whom I could spend the rest of my life?

His father had traits like my father did. Will Kzoo be anything like his father? It scares me. I don't want to expose children to that environment. There is no proof it would happen, and no proof it won't. Do I think he could be like that?

So what's the problem? I am afraid of the possibilities. Could he really love me? If I love him will I push him away? Only once I love him can he truly hurt me. Is it love I am afraid of? I can't be with a guy who doesn't love me. I hardly know him. I need time. Time can change a person. His hands are so amazing though. Holding his hand filled me with peace. Stop! It is too fast. I have to find it in myself first. I have to learn to trust and love myself before I can trust and love him.

Is it an option? Yes. I could wake up to him every morning, have him there when I go to sleep, hold him and be held all night long. I can feel the safety. I can feel him. I can still hear his words. A question I can't answer tonight.

Indecision continues to invade, the conversation has continued, it is now February 7th. There is a dual going on within me. My heart versus my head and my head has always won. Now I ponder faith. Faith is when we believe in something, when common sense tells you not to. Uncertainty has minimized. I can say I believe and trust in that. What's the worst that can happen? If I give him my heart the worst he can do is break it. I think I'm ready to take that chance.

That was not the conversation I was expecting. February 10th I called him. I think he just told me I'm going to hell. It's interesting how spirituality can be a common ground but religion can tear you apart. He said he can't marry someone who is not a Christian. If it's a choice between him and my faith I choose my faith. I cannot condemn anyone nor should you be able to predict my path to God. Clearly you don't want me, you want to change me. If what you say is true, that you love me. Do you love me for me or for what you intend my outcome to be? As I return the words and say I love you, know it is who you are today that I love, and not who you may become tomorrow. Just as you can't marry someone who isn't Christian, I don't think I can marry someone without an open mind, willing to accept the potential for psychic abilities, energy, reincarnation and direct communication with God. I'm not saying the guy I marry needs to understand it, but they must have an open mind to believe my connection with God is special and my experiences valid.

Amongst all the complex relationship stuff, trying to figure out what's going on with Sam, Joe and Kzoo, another person entered the picture. The early days had seemingly little significance at that moment in time, there were very few journal entries, but many saved emails. *It was the day before Valentine's Day 1997; I was at the Computer Centre working on my essay, when my screen went black. This DOS prompt pops up and some guy said "Hi... I am the large haired person that strolls about the Computer Centre. I have on occasion said a word or two to you; I believe Sugar Crisps was our last topic of discussion. :)"*

I looked around to see if I could find the guy I thought it was. "Who do you think you are and what happened to my work?" I had no idea what just happened, how he found me, how he took control of my screen, why it turned black and what happened to what I was working on, or how to get it back. Maybe I was a bit too rude. He returned my screen back to normal. Later I found an email in my inbox, he introduced himself as Eric. He said my eyes looked like I had something to say. Why do guys always comment on the eyes?

I spent Valentine's Day with Joe. It's crazy that as soon as he calls I go, but I love being with him so much. It never seems to matter what argument we may have had, we always end up together. I'll try not to think about it and just enjoy it while it lasts.

I think I found the source of my problems. Let it be known that February 16th 10:46am, I said the words; "God loves me." and a cold shiver ran through me.

"God loves me." I repeat the words again out loud and they are painful to hear. How? How can God love me? My own father didn't love me. I try to convince myself that I am loveable, but it's so hard. How could anyone love me? Emily does. I believe that.

I can't keep a guy for four weeks. Kzoo commented on my lack of a long term relationship. Maybe it's just that by week four I know it won't last! My head hurts so much tears stream down my face. I just want to be loved. Kzoo can't love me for me, though. Joe only calls when he wants something, the one boy I truly love. That's why it's so hard to let him go, because then I'll have nothing left. I'm so pathetic! There's got to be someone out there who is right for me! When will I be loved? God, I want to feel your love. I do. But everyone I love hurts me. I don't want to be hurt anymore. I don't want to be empty any more.

"You have to love yourself before anyone else can." Were those my words or God's?

So what do I like about me? I like my will to survive, my intuition, and my ability to find the good in any situation. I can dance, I can sing, I am determined and I care.

Friday, Feb 21st. Life got crazy. Some guy I've seen in the quiet study room and chatted with on a few occasions called and told me "I need to see you; I love you."

His voice sounded off. We weren't that close and never really talked outside of the quiet study room. "Um, I'm not sure what's going on. Are you ok?" I asked

He seemed intense. "I need to stay in Canada. I love you. You have to marry me."

I guess his student visa was expiring. He seemed to be in panic mode "I'm sorry. I can't marry you." I tried to be straightforward and honest.

"You have to marry me. I'm coming over now." he said. His voice turned from panicked to creepy.

"I don't want you to come over. I'm not going to marry you." I said. What else could I say?

"I'm coming now." he continued.

"How? You don't know where I live." I said, mildly confused.

"But I do." he corrected me. "I followed you home one day; you didn't see me."

"That's not ok. You can't follow me, stalk me or convince me to do something I don't want to do. I've told you I'm not interested. You need to accept that." Suddenly I was aware I was home alone and needed to address this quickly.

He then went on a psychotic soliloquy about how we'd live together and he'd get to stay in Canada.

There was only one way I was going to get him to listen to me. "Sure, you could come over," I started, "but the police would be here before you arrive."

I hung up and called campus police. He lived in a student residence, so I called their front desk and then the local police. I'm not afraid anymore!

February 24th. I had a crazy dream last night. I called Alistair and we talked for three hours. He told me a story about a sunset. It was beautiful. I wanted to hold him in my arms and I feel him near. We talked about us, and what's holding us together after so long. We talked about things in my life, opening my mind and all of my love and trust issues, as well as the people I love: Emily, him, Joe. We talked about everything, including how he doesn't really know me anymore and yet still knows me better than most people. I told him about the soul searching I've done, things I've learned and remembered from my early childhood. I told him everything on a general level, but I still told him.

We talked about why I called – all the memories that I've had of him recently, and that intense dream I had about him that turned into a fantasy. I felt so close to him. He is one of those guys whose arms I could peacefully fall asleep in. He talked of moments that he and I shared. He covered all my favourite moments.

"I could see us married." he said.

"You are someone I would seriously consider spending the rest my life with." I told him.

"I wish I could be with you now." he said.

"You are." I told him.

"I miss you." his words seemed to engulf me.

"You are sending butterflies to my stomach." I started, "You are like a warm security blanket I never want to let go." I feel so safe with him. I trust him. He returned the feelings.

It was 2:30 in the morning and call-waiting patched in. It was Sal, and I let him go. It messed up the moment, but it was ok. Alistair and I talked for a few more minutes.

"You've made my life more confusing. When will I talk to you again?" he asked.

"Saturday." I promised.

"I'll email you." he said.

"I don't want to let you go." I continued.

"Saturday. Take care Ang. Sweet dreams." I loved listening to his voice.

"Goodnight, Al, talk to you soon." My heart felt so full.

I miss Alistair. He is one whom I've loved and trusted for so long, and he knows everything. I crave that comfort. I crave that reciprocity. Why does he have to be so far away? I hear him talk of marriage and I am consumed. His words induce amazing feelings, so different than those from Kzoo. Yet again, almost a year later two guys are talking marriage.

I'm not including the creepy study room guy. This time, with Alistair, was the first time I thought of it and was filled with so much warmth and love. It was almost as if he was here with me physically, sending sensations to every part of my body.

February 27th. The "big-haired boy" Eric and I had sent a few emails back and forth, mostly about why he was emailing me, loaded with sarcasm. I've seen him at the Computer Centre and have had a few interactions. He seems innocent, kid-like and harmless. Today Eric sent me a genuine, sarcasm-free email. I've decided to include it, considering in hindsight how much of an impact it had. His email was philosophical, offered insight, and made me want to talk to him.

> *Good Morning Angela, I begin this letter with the promise that there will be no sarcasm in anything that I say. After all, it is my time of the night right now. You asked for something that I loved and well, tonight is a perfect example of what I love.*
>
> *There is a house, where everyone is asleep, silence in the halls, silence everywhere. Darkness lives just outside the light of my door and the sound of falling rain floods what thirsts of silence. And there is an eerie calm in myself and there is an extension of myself into myself that makes me feel whole, if even for a moment. I sit here, calm and relaxed, aware and silent, listening and watching thoughts float by, catching and viewing them for a moment, sometimes two moments, and letting them drift further on. Contemplation, worry and fear are not around, just simple glancing thoughts that keep existence and its trials at arms' reach.*
>
> *This is one of my loves, this silence. But, it's the silence that actually brings to life my second love, and that is my writing. I dabble a little in the idea that I can write, that I have the power of word and expression, as if to claim that I have ability to show to some the state of being, of mind, of existence, as seen through the eyes of its author.*

That is a love of mine, to leave behind some state, some written reference of a moment that was who I was. Much like now, these words that I write to you, hold form of who I am, for the moment I wrote these words.

>Angela wrote: I have no problem with your name; I actually think it's interesting (he had the same name as Kzoo). I also checked out your home page :)

Which name is interesting, Eric or Fozzie? (Honest question). Also, you checked out my homepage, eeek. That's not good. My page sucks :(I wish I had known. I would have cleaned it up before. :) <

>>Eric wrote: It seems important to me, however, to state that it is the simple things and the things that we seem to take for granted, of those things that we take as obvious, or useless; where so much exists. <<

>Angela wrote: Just wanted to let you know I took this totally out of context and oddly applied it to my life. Then I started thinking: have you realized we talk without really saying anything? After four emails, I still hardly know anything about who you are, what you like, what you do in your spare time, how you feel about things, what you love most, what you hate most, or the most important things that ever happened in your life. I know nothing. <

As stated before, my letters had been sort of designed with this method of simple conversing without divulgence of myself, for fear that upon viewing the one that writes these letters you'd choose not to respond. It's easier to converse when the conversation is not on self, is it not?

But I agree, there is much that I don't know of you either, things that I simply must infer based on these writings and minimal personal contact with you.

My likes are simple. (As to what this means, it is not clear- just that complex thought is something I enjoy, but the thoughts on the simple things are more enjoyable. [*I'm not sure this says what I mean.*]) In my spare time, I like coffee with friends, hanging out with friends, talking, and meeting new people (like you).

What I love most and what I hate most are perhaps the same thing. I love my writings and the way my writings feel and live; but I hate the way they take of me and the desire that seems to drive me to write. (Perhaps this is the same of many who are writers [*although I am not a qualified writer.*]). Actually, as I read this over, I suppose my hate is no longer as stressed, since I no longer feel driven to write.

The most important thing to happen in my life, I think in many parts would have to be the realization of my mortality, the acceptance of my mortality, the attainment of appreciation of life, the development of appreciation of the simple things. And yes, these can stem from one event (although groundwork indeed was laid out years before this). The event of course, was hitting bottom in my life and the realization of how stupid it was. It's a long story, but well, depression (and my subsequent testing and manipulations of depressions) has served as a major turning point in my life, for the reason of finding total self and a power within.

Hmmm, perhaps I'm going too much into telling of who I am now. But I will continue, since I still feel fairly comfortable in continuing.

>Angela wrote: I've tried, but how many times can you say, sure all this crap has happened, but I'm still going to stop and look at the sky and look at how beautiful it is on this clear night. Yeah, the beauty and the vastness of the unknown only minimize my life further and ever-so-nicely points out that I shouldn't be upset-worried-frustrated... I'm only one person in a world of eternity... you know how small we are if you compare us to the universe, so how much can what's going on in my life really matter? Yeah, the simple things, many people have tried, but before one can appreciate the

so-called simple things in life, one has to be able to take life at face value and open their mind up enough to take in the environment. One thing that has always been able to clear my mind was the night sky, for under it I know I am not alone… unless of course it's cloudy and I fear that my true family may be coming to pick me up and won't be able to find me if there's a cloud cover, but hey, if they can find earth in the collection of masses out there, of course they could find me on a skimpy little planet like earth. <

I don't mean to sound surprised, rather in awe. WOW! I like this paragraph, this passage. But I question why it is that you look to the clear night sky. Sure the stars are there, and the sky fills you with the awesome array of points of light, so distant, yet so tangible. And the occasional shooting star that streaks its way across the upper atmosphere almost makes you believe that if you tried hard enough that you could reach them and hold one for your own. (I'm from the country, and, well, I've lain under the sky many nights in awe of the black night sky speckled with stars).

But I find the cloudy nights and the rainy dreary days so much brighter. When the sun shines and the sky is blue, or the millions of stars shine down, it seems so obvious it is beauty. It seems so obvious that there is beauty out there and because of this obviousness, you know that it is not you alone that sees it. But when the clouds block out the moon and the stars, can you see the beauty in knowing or realizing that the stars still shine on? Realize that when a cloud breaks and one shines through that it's fought to be there, or that you fought to see it there. Even though you cannot see the beauty, underneath the cloak, the skin, the cover; there is the beauty you knew. In the falling rain, there comes new life and an end to a cycle that will only begin again.

These are the simple things, these realizations of the continuance of existence in beauty, and the need to not always have to hold sight of it, grasp on, for its existence is truly reason to be. And once you see the beauty – with knowledge that there is beauty – even where it cannot be seen, this leads to a greater ability to accept the many things of life. Every demon, every hardship leads the way to some grandness because of it. Like appreciating or loving more, that single star that breaks the cloud-filled sky.

>Angela wrote: Hmmm :) Would this happen to be an invite to meet up? <

Perhaps, better put, I should make this a request. I have grown more intrigued. I always enjoy a good discussion, and certainly just from the things you have written in this and those other letters, I believe it would be fun (to me anyway). This happens to be one of my loves, the discussion of ideas of many things, in the quest for some greater understanding. (Oh, I just remembered a hate of mine: people that appear false. I.E., those shallow people who pretend to be what they are not, for some selfish goal – I mention this because I felt for a moment that it may seem that I am saying these things to impress you or others, as opposed to what they really are, my true view.)

>Angela wrote: Also taken fully out of context. Our childhoods were likely very different. I don't think, as a child, things were any simpler…if anything they were much more difficult. As it happens, I believe I've forgotten anything that was simple during my childhood. Every story has a memory, none of them too innocent. <

I did not mean to claim life then was simpler, just that in looking back with our aged minds and understanding of more complex things, we look back and realize that the things we had challenge us as a child pale in comparison to those that we seem to face now (just as in some future time, the trials of now will pale to those of the future). Indeed, there is much difficulty as a child because those things that we learned and formed as a foundation make up who we became. (I have a theory to this regard which I will share when I have more time and space).

>Angela wrote: So tell me something interesting about your life… <

Not sure I have succeeded in this through the course of this letter, but I have tried to portray myself as I am. I suppose it is up to you to decide whether it was interesting.

This week has been strange though. I don't think I've spent the entire night at home yet. I am always going out to watch movies or play euchre. Hmmm, you play euchre? If you do, perhaps I'll try to invite you into a game sometime. But certainly, if you want, I would love to engage you in some form of one on one conversation. I may be in computer science, but as long as I can remember I have been claimed to being a deep person (philosophically), and I find a home in analyzing human behaviour through real life models. Perhaps we'll go for coffee one day and talk?

Um, eeek, it's 5:20am. I believe this means that I should have been in bed already. I'm not sure how large this message is, but forgive the length. I tend to be long-winded this early in the morning, but also very talkative.

Awaiting response to invite,

Eric

PS: I hope you enjoyed this sarcasm free letter. Or at least I believe it is, I feel tired and strange right now. Night!

So the email changed things. I saw him at the Computer Centre shortly after and we started talking. The face to face conversations began. The sarcasm was disappearing, the interactions were awkward, childish and a bit slow, but we both knew there was something deeper to work towards…

Saturday March 1st, 1997. Well, um, ok. I spent last night at Joe's. I don't know what power this guy has over me; he flips my mind so fast away from any other guy. He is amazing! Two and a half hours of amazing! That guy's got my body, head and heart. I don't know how to slow down when it comes to him.

"*I love you.*" *I told him.*

"*I like you a lot,*" *he responded,* "*I don't want to lose what we have.*"

I know it is the way Joe works. But it's so hard to not feel the loss. What do we have? Is it just an open relationship? I need more than just sex. Is that what he doesn't want to lose?

I know we have an amazing connection, trust, security, and great sex. It's all there and he just won't talk about emotions. I need the emotional connection validated and he won't go there. I need more than "I like you a lot."

I called Alistair. We talked about how our relationship progressed and our last night before I left for University. As much as we are connected emotionally, when he talks about seeing us married, my thoughts focus on the distance. Alistair and I are in different cities and will be for a while. I want to be with him, but he's so far away. I would need to be physically next to him. If only I could merge the emotional and stable relationship mindset of Alistair with all of Joe's assets and find my perfect guy.

March 2ⁿᵈ. I had another amazing night with Joe. I told him about the open honest conversations I've had with Alistair and Eric. We stayed up late talking about trust and love. He said "I want to be like Data *from* Star Trek *and feel nothing."*

"*That would be a lonely world.*" *I said.* "*You were the one that taught me I could trust. I hadn't fully trusted anyone new since all the crap with my dad. You were the one that made me realize that some people are worth exposing yourself to that vulnerability.*" *I'm not sure what's going on with him. The emotional stuff we had seems to be disappearing.*

I saw Eric at the Computer Centre today, March 3ʳᵈ. He initiated a chat on the computer, but I finally convinced him to go for a walk. It was our first real conversation. I like the sarcasm-free version of him so much more.

March 6ᵗʰ. What a rollercoaster of a week. I don't know where I'm headed or what I'm doing, but my brain hurts. I saw Joe with someone else. I don't want to hurt any more. If I mean anything to him he shouldn't be with other people when he's with me. What would I say to him? The relationship could stay the same; I just need to know he's not out there having sex with other people?

WHAT DID I JUST DO? I don't know. He said, "I'll get back to you on that." Great. Why did I do that? I needed to. Why couldn't I let the relationship heal a bit before I threw that at him? Meanwhile I'm just another person turning on him, destroying him that much more. What have I done? I just can't deal with this anymore. He either wants to be with me (only me) or it's over. Either way, I feel more at peace that there may be an end to the roller coasters. Are these feelings pointless, the feeling that I needed him to myself? I can't be the other girl anymore. So, I initiated another big fight just before his birthday? What did I just do? I'm such an ass, a horrible friend. I feel like crap. But it has to stop. I can't continue this way and if his answer is in the negative, as I fully expect it to be, maybe I can finally move on.

I'm sad. It's March 11th and I feel so alone. No one understands me. I feel like crying, my head aches. I am so sick of pain. Why doesn't anyone love me? Why do I have to be so lonely? I try reading, it's a quick fix, but it doesn't last. Nothing lasts. I can feel love is near, but it presents as physical gratification. That is not love. I need love.

March 12th. Joe wrote me. "It is probably worthwhile that you look out for your own interests, no matter how misplaced, confounding and perplexing it is for they that are at the receiving end of such crass and brazen effrontery. I bear no grudge; your nature is human. Nevertheless, a simple birthday wish would have been comforting. Forget I ever existed. I remain."

So I responded... "First of all I can never forget that you exist. Many times that phone ended up in my hand on your birthday, I couldn't press the last number. 'I'll get back to you.' Echoes. Joe, I love you! That's something that will never change. But it hurts too much to be so close to you physically, believing the feelings will always be one-way. The words 'I like you a lot' stung. I tried; perhaps not hard enough, perhaps with the wrong words. But it couldn't remain the way it was, that I know. It's probably all I know right now. Besides, I don't ever want you out of my life. You bear no grudge, yet I ask forgiveness."

13

Dealing with Rape

My mind, struggling to get back to the present, the next token memory was the salt package. It lay tucked in nicely amongst so many happier memories. Joe's liquor label and Sam's dime fit snugly together, flattening the salt package against the inside of that Black Ice beer bottle cap. Rape – it was nestled in there amongst the best date ever and two amazing friends, almost as if the position would lessen the sting. It was the only time in my life I've ever blacked out.

It was March 15th, 1997, and I was studying at the Students' Centre, chatting on and off with a few of the regulars. I had seen him many times, even studied at the same table and chatted. He seemed like someone I'd be friends with. We talked about basic stuff; it seemed casual and didn't raise any alarms. It was getting late, so I started packing up to go home. He said he was leaving too, so we walked together. He walked me home and then came in. I don't know what we were talking about or how he negotiated his way into my house, or up to my room for that matter. All of those memories were swept away in my tequila induced blackout.

I do remember that we ended up in my room and he became way too physical. I told him to stop. He didn't; he undressed me. I yelled. He still didn't stop. He worked his way inside me, similar to my childhood memories. He was at side of the bed, holding me down. I was immobilized by my past and my present. I started crying and somehow managed to kick him off. I grabbed my clothes and ran to the washroom. I needed safety. Liz was home. I went downstairs and knocked on her door. She said she was busy watching a movie. Orville was over. Hadn't they heard me? Couldn't they have stopped it? That night I was violated, by more than one person.

Help me! *I need a friend right now! Becky (a good friend from residence) was home. I brought a bottle of tequila. We finished it. I kept one of the salt packets to represent my lowest moment. How could I not have seen the warnings? How could it get that far in my home? Fear quickly turned to anger. I don't know how that happened. You like power, you like control, but I'm not going to let you make a victim out of me. Maybe that's what I needed to gain full respect of my body once again. I had no idea what I was getting into. I feel so invaded, so dirty.*

Becky wants me to go to the police do the swab and toss him in jail. All I could think about was my childhood. How can it happen again years later? Becky and I met up with Mike; he's one I've always felt safe with. I know he will protect me tonight. Mike wants to know who did it; he said he'd beat the crap out of the guy. I just wanted a drink and to forget it all. This was the first time I ever drank enough to black out. I knew they would get me home safely and they did.

Swoosh

All the curtains close.
Click.
Every light goes out.
Blackness.
It absorbs me.
Thick heavy satin.
It covers me.
The dark shadows make me one.
Angela, 1997

Years later, I learned that beta blockers are sometimes given to rape victims, which can greatly reduce their emotional attachment to the event, if given in a timely manner at rape clinics. The beta blockers numb the emotions and reduce the chances of post-traumatic stress disorder. It made me wonder: did the intense drinking and blackout that night have a similar effect? Am I better than I could have been? Either way, I am eternally grateful to Becky and Mike for being there and keeping me safe that night.

I think the impact of rape and abuse has everything to do with body memory; the specific position brought back everything. That was why I needed Joe, to clear away the memories of this rape. I knew Joe would find the good spots and do a good job. He is aware of my past and would be completely ok if I broke down in the middle of it. For me, sex after rape needs to happen quickly. I have to erase what happened. But Joe and I aren't talking. I have to fix that.

March 16th. I tried calling Joe, but he hasn't talked to me since the last email March 12th. The call was a mistake. He gave me a lesson in talking and he's so right. I never thought about the way I laid everything out for him and how it must have made him feel. I was self-centred, egotistical, and simply rude. Fine. I was raped and need you now more than ever! *I couldn't tell him. This call wasn't about me.*

Amanda occupied my next few nights at the pub. I got all my "angry girl" songs out and evidently impressed the DJ again; she offered to do a few duets. Would being a lesbian be any easier? At least I've got Amanda, Becky, and my karaoke buddy, as well as Mike on my side, all willing to protect me against anything.

I became very slow to respond to everyone else. *My protective emotional walls are now higher than they've ever been. How do I let anyone in? Who do I let in? How do I start talking to people again? How do I keep myself safe? What warning signs do I look for? My incoherent words on instant messaging with Eric the day after I was raped seemed to change things. He knew something had happened; I was saying something without saying anything.*

March 21st. I saw Eric at the Computer Centre early this morning. He emailed me and wrote "I must say, I have always enjoyed (not always understood, but enjoyed) talking to you (and will continue to), but currently and for some time I am not on a quest for a relationship (past a friendship). But I wonder how cliché that sounds, even when it is truth."

Eric called around 2:30am and we talked for six hours. It started great, but ended in a way that left me feeling deflated. He told me that people who really know him are weaknesses and he doesn't need any more of those. I feel so alone and isolated right now. I need someone whom I feel safe with; perhaps I've said too much.

March 26th. I had a very interesting conversation last night which got my mind off of my stuff. Eric called around one in the morning. We talked until six in the morning and I'm glad we did. It was interesting. He read me a poem that was darker than I would have expected. The conversation went dark and deep and negative and then so easily developed sexual connotations. Conversations with him are so dynamic, with all emotions covered. It was funny, weird and entertaining, and by the time we said goodbye I had forgotten about almost all of the negative stuff previously said. I crazily wanted to thank him for letting me into his life.

March 28th. Emily thankfully came to visit. I needed my sister. We just hung out and she helped me forget about everything going on. Together we went to see Joe. He was happy to see Emily and it was almost two hours before he realized he was still mad and wasn't talking to me. Anyway, it worked and we are cool again. He agreed to meet up with me on Sunday after she leaves. Joe is the only one I trust enough to be that vulnerable with. I don't know what will happen when he touches me. I don't know what I will say or do. But I've had flashbacks with him before. He can handle my trauma. He has heard my stories and comforted me. I know he could again if needed.

March 31st. I finally got together with Joe last night and yet, for the first time, I didn't feel I could tell him what happened. I kept the stories silent. There have been too many fights lately, too many ups and downs. I just needed him for the critical task of cleansing my body of all the bad memories. I used Joe. I needed to. I couldn't handle the thoughts of the last one who touched me, continuing to poison my body. I needed to use him to get over my trauma, without telling him what or why. It was awkward. He knew it was awkward. But it worked, and by the end of it I felt I could breathe again. Taking my body back and choosing to have sex, enjoying sex and feeling pleasure being with someone I love and trust was enough to stop the poison and start the healing. I love Joe for being there; I will never forget what he did for me today.

Know me

Know me then, but you never will,
The sweet hello's of the daffodil.
The smiling eyes, the fearless face,
The undreamt dreams of life with lace.
Know me before traumas that killed,
The scars that made thoughts unwilled.
Before the tears, before the pain,
Before the fear, before the drain.
Remember me, the loving girl,
Whose face was framed in a pretty curl.
The carefree me you'll never know,
Who stayed to watch the lilies grow.
You know me now, wrinkles and grey,
Changed by stories; I regret to say.
It was the silent day, when the air grew cold,
The dark sky came, that I grew old.
If you knew me then you'd know now why,
It feels like I've already died.
The clouds roll in, it's time to go,
But I am not now who you'll never know.

Angela, 1997

Sometimes talking to a therapist is the necessary type of communication. I had many therapists over the years. *Today we talked a lot about Albert Ellis, a cognitive behavioural theorist. His basic theory was that there were ABC's to every event. You have no control over the A – action. But you can choose your B - behaviour which in turn forms your C – consequence. I hadn't looked at my issues like that before. I choose how to respond to what happened. An event is not over until I've decided it is over. We talked a lot about my rape. He was the one who got me the morning after pill and went at my speed when talking to figure out what I wanted to do about it. I want to confront my rapist. I wanted to confront my childhood abuser, but realized that nothing would come of it. He's old now and would not learn. I likely couldn't stop him from doing it again. The guy from the quiet study room had potential to at least consider what happened and think about what he was doing and maybe listen next time someone said stop. I don't know if it will make a difference but I think by confronting him, I could let the memories of my childhood molester stop affecting me.*

I remember I got in so much trouble one year when I opened a present from my Grandma, it was a dress. She commented on how pretty she thought it was so I told her she could keep it. My mom said my response was rude and uncalled-for. But I was terrified: didn't they know my abuser was in the room? He liked dresses. I didn't.

14

Finding Happiness

*T*he heart came out of a friendship candle one night Eric and I were on the phone for over five hours. The more time I spent talking to him, the more my heart healed. I have other token memories, but this one best defines our early days.

April 4th 1997. Ok, so Eric, "Mr. I don't want a relationship" did a double take this morning. "I surprised you." I said with a questioning smile as I noticed him.

"Yeah, you look good today." he said.

"And…that surprised you?" I asked, laughing.

"Well I just had to do a double take; I wasn't expecting it." he responded, clearly stumbling to recover from his unintentional behaviour.

"What, me looking half-decent?" I asked. He was being cute; we ended up going for a walk.

When I got home, he called me and we had another interesting conversation. This one was a tad different from our previous calls with quite a few innuendos. I'm having a tough time wiping this smile off of my face. I don't know. Perhaps it was this morning when he told me I looked good like ten times on our walk, or when he said "I'm sorry I got sidetracked when you got to showering." The idea of "naked" just kept coming up in the conversations. Perhaps the smile started when he said "just by answering the phone, you put my mind in the gutter."

We also talked a lot about "friendships" and that there are three categories that people usually fit into and most know where they are. The first is not even really a friend, but someone you recognize and chat with occasionally. The second category is purely friends, simple and sweet. Then there are those I consider to be much more than friends, guys who I like and who know it.

"So where do I fit in," he asked, "between the last two?"

"I guess…" I started.

"Then you've totally blown your theory." he quickly interjected.

"But you're an exception. You can't be classified as a just a friend, because you know too much information." I replied.

"Yeah I guess you'd be the same." There was a pause before he continued, "So now you have to add a fourth category."

"No way, that would allow other people to get in there. I think you'll just have to remain an outlier." It was more complementary than I intended, but it was there and flowed smoothly.

We ended up talking all night; it was about 8:30am when we finally hung up. But the relationship aspect has yet to change. I guess we are waiting for his readiness to enter one. As far as getting to know him and becoming a weakness, like he said on March 21st, I think we've surpassed that.

April 6th. After talking all night again on the phone, including discussions about our thoughts and feelings towards each other, we started talking about what it would be like when we next saw each other. "Why wait?" he said, likely just wanting to get off of the phone after the eight hour discussion.

"Hmm, you want me to come over?" I asked.

It was less than a ten minute walk. We continued the conversation in person, this time starting with a big hug. He was still apprehensive about our relationship and moving forward, but we are officially dating. It was interesting though: he won't let me kiss him. He wants to find the perfect moment.

Today is April 9th. Eric and I were in the Students' Centre studying when I saw a face that made me freeze. It was the first sighting since that night he raped me. My initial response of fear, and being immobilized by memories quickly turned to anger and hate. I remembered my mom finding her strength and ending the abuse, the power it took to address the abuse and face the unknown.

I tried to harness her power, feel it, be empowered by it, address my abuser and face the unknown. Momentarily grounded enough to act, I asked Eric if I could borrow him. He's six foot two and a perfect body guard. Shaking, I asked Eric to stay at the end of the aisle. He was ready to help if needed, and I walked up to my abuser, trembling, wanting to throw up, wanting to hit him, wanting to run away. I focused on my mom. I focused on the ABC's. I choose my behaviour which forms my consequences. I choose my future. I can do this. I opened my mouth and the words found their way out.

"Do you realize what you did to me?" I asked him. "You are lucky I didn't go to the police. I clearly said no and you kept going. I did not want to have sex with you. You should have stopped when I said stop!" He looked down the aisle at Eric, and said nothing. I walked away feeling I was going to collapse in a nervous adrenaline rush. I couldn't stop shaking. Eric took me for a walk to regain my composure. I'm so glad he was there for me. Man I love tall guys! It was getting easier to talk, and his being there for me today created an instant trust bond. I told him more about what happened that night.

April 10*th*. My dreams, my hopes, they are so distorted. What I love most is being loved and feeling wanted. And why is this so difficult? I don't know. I have so much to do, so much studying, so much reading, and yet here I sit with my journal, thinking and pondering over boys. I got an email from Joe. He wrote "I have to tell you something before we talk."

I called to ask, "What's going on?"

"I started seeing someone." he told me.

"That's great." I said. "Can you imagine us together as friends, without a physical relationship? Is that possible? I'd love to try."

I know nothing and that is all I know. It is crazy to think I may never have sex with Joe again. It is crazy how quickly a world can change. That ultimatum was needed, poorly-executed, and yet Joe was still there for me when I needed him. Then just like that, it's over. Joe and I will never be exclusive, but Eric will, and right now I need the safety of exclusivity.

I had a great time with Eric last night, just in his room, talking, studying. It was almost morning, I needed to go to sleep and he offered his bed for me to rest. I knew I had to go home to get some good sleep. As I got up to leave, he was standing right in front of me. He was finally going to do it. He gently touched my face and then cupped it in both hands. Looking into my eyes, inhaling with anticipation, he kissed me. It was perfect.

April 17*th*. I love that we can lie together all night and just hug. I love talking to you. I love the safety I feel in your arms. I love that you listen to me and don't judge. I love that you want to spend as much time with me as I do with you. I love that when you read your poems that I can feel the power behind them. I love that we can understand each other's minds. Most of all, I hope that things with you are different.

April 18*th*. Joe called. He's on his way. We are supposed to talk tonight. I feel so nervous. Can I do this? Talk to him as a friend? Why is this so hard? I love Joe. He knows it. I know it. Eric knows it. Eric went home for the weekend, but will be back for my birthday. Tonight will be a major test, a test of strength, growth, and my feelings towards Eric.

He just left: it is 4:18am, and he was here for almost four hours. Each time Joe walks out my door a part of me leaves too. My heart saddens every time he walks away. We were talking about different stages in our lives and relationships and what happened when and why. I gave him a letter I wrote to him back in September:

Joe, I've yet to decide as to whether or not this letter will ever reach your hands, but here it goes. I miss you. Lots! I don't care if we are friends... more than... less than... It's just that when you walked away, it felt so final. I'm curious as to what you heard and why you want to come over, but I'm guessing the severity must be fairly bad. Yes, I want to know what your thoughts are and what's bothering you. I hope one day you'll be able to talk to me again.

I know lots of what's going on presently is my fault. I left with a challenge on my mind and did great. I went through summer and did nothing more than kiss one boy, an ex. I was constantly thinking about you. I'm sorry. I guess I didn't really know what I was getting into. I fell for you. I fell harder than I've ever fallen for anyone in my entire life. You are the only guy out there whom I fully trust. Trust with me is a big thing. I'm sorry I said the things I said. I care for you greatly and I don't want you to walk out of my life. "I know I could face the bitter cold but life without you, I don't know." (Celine Dion.)

I don't know what to do. You are my best friend and more, my only constant last year. You were easy to talk to and your touches were comforting. My heart breaks a little each day I don't see you. My instinct could be right and you may never return.

I love your eyes, smile, and touch. I guess I just love you!

Angela

He read it then kissed me. I pulled away. "I'm with somebody now." I said.

"I don't care." he said and kissed me again.

"I do." I told him, and pulled back a second time. "You have indirectly broken up every relationship I've entered since I met you."

"It's your fault for being so pretty." he said.

"We need to end the physical stuff." I said. He hugged me. This was the first time in months that we were alone together and did not have sex. We talked about all of this emotional stuff I've seemingly waited forever for him to say.

"It doesn't matter who I'm with because you were before them and will be after them and for the last two years you have always been my constant." he told me.

"And you, mine." I said, "Joe, I love you. You will always carry a special place in my heart."

"I'm afraid I'll lose you." he said.

"You won't." I told him.

"I already have." he said, the sadness held in the eye contact was heart breaking.

Four hours he was here. I feel I am losing a part of myself. My spirit and his are intermingled, we are only whole when together. But every time I ended my relationships to be with him, it always went the same way. He wasn't ready to be exclusive. With so much love, the absence is devastatingly heartbreaking. I can't continue to deal with the lows that follow such highs. How can I love someone so much? I miss him already.

May 26th. I've been dating Eric since Sunday, April 6th. After we "formalized" our love physically, I stopped keeping track of everything and decided to just let it go. I love waking up next to him and have on many occasions. Recently, we've been talking more about our futures. I think that was mostly instigated by a dream I had. It was him and I, years from now. We woke up together and were just lying in bed when he told me he wanted a baby. Awake and beside him, I thought, yeah, but will we? Eric said "Yes."

I hadn't told him the dream and wasn't talking out loud, but merely thinking to myself. Then, I thought "Was he was reading my mind?" Again he responded without my thoughts being voiced, only seconds after the mental question.

So our day continued and I decided to ask "Would it scare you if I said I could see myself spending the rest of my life with you?"

He said "No." and told me thoughts he had had of us. I told him about my dream and his coincidental unprompted responses that went along with my thoughts

June 7th. All major stories are out. He knows them all. I love him so much; he's great to be with, emotionally, physically, mentally and sexually. He knows my stories, triggers, what to watch for and would never let me get to a place where nasty memories could arise. He is the best of Alistair and Joe combined. We tried Alistair's breathless kiss. It was something he described to me once that sounded amazing. It's now officially my favourite kiss. The idea is that you breathe each other's air. It starts with our mouths open, me breathing in through my mouth as he breathes out through his. His breath enters my body, a part of him travelling deeper inside, reaching, caressing, touching me in places untouchable, and all of it done simultaneously. The first few breaths align inhales with exhales, but as it quickens the rhythm improves until I am breathing at his will. With each breath there is less and less oxygen, so breathing becomes heavier, incredibly intense and passionate.

Everything was new, fresh and untainted. Lately, we've been talking about two main topics: always and comfort levels. I went through a phase of asking myself; could I be with him and only him? I no longer question my abilities. I want to be with him always. He still gives me butterflies and makes me feel great about who I am. As for comfort levels, he seems to enjoy my adventurous streak: the swings, the library, the porch, yet always concealed, actions unknown to any who may pass by.

We talked about the future and where we'd want to live, dwellings, locations and kids. He asked "What would you say if I asked you to be with me always?"

I hesitated. "I'm not sure... I'd probably say yes... um... I think I'd say yes... No. I know, yeah, I'd say yes."

He looked at me almost laughing, leaned over and kissed me. I love him, truly, madly, and deeply.

So here I am, past the two month milestone I've never seemed to be able to achieve. I seem to have done all the tests, told all my stories, explored physically, and attachment to him is still growing. We've started talking about a future and after evaluating all those whom I've considered spending my life with... It's strange to be here and not find a reason to back out or question what is going on. Maybe this is it.

June 15*th*. It's now 3:08am and it's kind of weird, but I miss Eric lots. I'm sad because he went home for the weekend. I went out with Liz tonight and had a good time, I guess. It's been a weird day. We saw Sam, his friend tried picking me up and I told him that I have a boyfriend. Sam overheard this and, well, he then became quite curious about if I was telling the truth and who the guy is. It felt weird, his seemingly being jealous.

Also today, while babysitting, I thought a lot about the future aspect of my relationship. Eric and I have just been talking about it a lot lately and I guess it kind of scared me when he asked what I would say if he asked if I would be with him always. I've just been thinking about everything that question contained. Hailey was playing outside and I started wondering what it would be like if we had a little one running around. What would it be like to wake up to him every morning for the rest of my life? An odd sense of peace and comfort covered me as I was rocking her to sleep.

Tuesday I awoke to a huge lip and a saddened mood. It all just seemed to ambush me. Alas, it wasn't only the cold sore and the sense of inadequacy, but everything came up at once: the correlations, the situations, Father's Day, my dad's birthday and more. Eric provided much-needed comfort and at first it was difficult to accept. I couldn't imagine how he could possibly see me as anything other than the ugliness that I saw in myself at that point in time. His continuous comforting words convinced me my thoughts were unfounded. He later walked me home, and met Joe. It was *awkward, unexpected, yet interesting. The three of us talked for a bit, but I had to go to class. They left and I showered. Later I went to meet up with Eric at the pub, and met some of his friends. I love flirting and I love dancing. At the end of the night he walked me home in his bare feet. It was so cute: weird, but cute.*

15

Personal Growth

The dolphin represents freedom and choice. I was walking past a display at the Students' Centre and it called to me. I often held it to remind myself to slow down and make deliberate choices. My worst housemate lived in the room next to me at Amanda's and instigated a few of my personal growth lessons. This girl often had friends over and was loud well past midnight. Her college exam schedules were different from ours and she was incredibly disrespectful during our exam periods. I think my problem with her was a combination of hypocrisy and entitlement. She came from money and believed she deserved it. She had failed out of many schools and had "Daddy" pay for everything. He gave her a $1000 spending money each month after he paid for her rent, car, tuition and books. Yet she would always be the first to complain that she had no money.

April, 1997. *Tonight, after Amanda and I had finished our exams, we had gone to the bar and come home with two new friends. We thought it was due payback. This roommate walked in asked us to turn the music down. We turned it up. She yelled at us. I thought some pretty nasty thoughts at her. She woke up late the next morning, I heard her panic and went back to sleep thinking she deserved it. I woke up at 9:02am feeling unsettled and reflected that I shouldn't have had such mean thoughts. When she got home, she complained about the horrific morning she had. She said she was almost creamed by another car, but she swerved and it stopped just inches from her car. I looked at her and said I was sorry.*

"For what?" she asked, looking stunned.

"I cursed you, but this morning I felt bad and lifted it at 9:02." I said.

"That's when I was almost hit." she said.

"I know." I responded. "I'm sorry."

The colour seemed to drain out of her face. I was serious and sincere. Liz and Amanda, however, capitalized on this event to remind our roommate I was a witch and could cause her harm if she didn't smarten up. This event dramatically changed her behaviour. She became respectful of our schedules and tolerable to live with, but she did move out to live with her new college friends in the fall.

Secretly, the event scared me. I suddenly saw the correlation between the people in my family and all the accidents that happened. Of course, all the events are random, but can negative thoughts really have such an impact? Does dark magic exist? We don't have slow, natural death in my family, but rather it seems all the guys die following intense arguments or resentment. My grandmother was the only female who died. One family member was hit and killed by a drunk driver. One killed himself with an overdose. Another killed himself with a gun. My father was murdered. There is only one male still alive from my blood family and he has had had two strokes and many sporadic life-threatening injuries, but always seems to live!

I called a spiritual advisor to help figure stuff out. I have had prophetic dreams for years and taught myself to read palms and cards. I'd projected positive energy before, but never had the negative projections been so powerful.

"I printed your charts earlier this week," she said, "I've never seen anything like them. You are at a crossroads in your life." Instantly, I *dismissed everything she had said.*

I believe every day is a crossroads. I thought she was giving me the run-of-the-mill speech.

"You need to focus and channel your energies, not just mentally, but physically too. Hold up your hands." she told me.

I did. She pushed energy at me, and my palms felt a force I can only describe as similar to the feeling of the repulsion when you try to push two magnets with reverse polarity together. But my hands were the other magnet and the sensation was full of warmth, pouring into my hands, filling my body with energy.

She then said, "You are so strong you could probably do it yourself. Put your hands up a few inches apart and be aware of your space. Feel the energy come up out of the ground, through your feet, body and hands."

Boom! Like a light switch, my energy was turned on. Now with each of my hands feeling like those magnets, I moved them ever so slightly and could feel the energy in the space between. I could push my hands together, and as I did that the energy force got stronger. I could hold it, feel it, push it through my hand and feel it on the other side. Amazing!

She spent a lot of time talking about my astrology chart and the number of past life regressions I had. "I've never seen anyone with so many. You must be a very old soul. Think about your experiences. Are there any experiences that seemed strange or paranormal?"

I told her about the tooth dreams and the warning dreams I've had.

"Write down your dreams, and you'll likely find more connections." she told me. "It is time to figure out what you want out of life and to work towards that goal."

What a loaded task, to figure out what I want…Well, I guess in the simplest terms, I want love, happiness, and to not have to worry about money. I'm sick of drama. I'm sick of all this crap. I want to work towards boring. I want to have enough money to buy what I need and most of my wants. I want to love and be loved equally. I want people to be honest and trustworthy. I am sick of deception and mind games. I want honest communication, no more secrets.

I started listening to my dreams more intently, and writing them down. *Last night I dreamt about that friend from high school whom I had found in the band room bathtub with her wrists slit. In my dream she was in another room calling for help. I woke up and could still hear her calling. I phoned her and told her about my dream.*

"I bought a lot of ecstasy for my birthday; I just feel like no one cares. I need an escape." she told me.

"It seems like you are calling for help. I don't think ecstasy is the answer."

We talked for an hour, put together a plan of things she could do, and she flushed the drugs. It seems like when those I care for are in need I can sense it. Yet I never seemed to get the same warnings for myself.

I needed a break from life and went to visit Emily. We decided to celebrate our birthdays with a hot air balloon ride. *We woke up really late, paid the cabbie double to get us there as fast as he could and dealt with the adrenaline rush of potentially missing it and not getting our money back. They were still filling up the balloon when we arrived 20 minutes* late. The liftoff was amazing! We floated up through the air and watched the sun rise. Gently soaring over fields and farms, life seemed to pause to allow full absorption of the beauty. Being with Emily always made things seem better, knowing we've survived worse; my daily woes were gone as that balloon lifted up.

August 10th. I am happy and very much in love. I've been with Eric just over four months and I love it. I can't seem to get enough of him. I don't know. I try to figure out if this is the same as the rest, or if this is different. I hope it is different. I think it is. Is he the one with whom I am going to spend the rest of my life? I love him so much and feel so comfortable with him. I feel like this is what I've been waiting for. I love him so much. I can see him in the rest of my life.

September 28th. I don't really know what to say, it's just been a weird day. I love being with Eric. I guess it was weird because Matt came to visit. And, well, I was told by a roommate that he likes me. It was that obvious to others? She asked why I don't go for him. My immediate response was "I love Eric."

I simply couldn't find a space for any other guy in my thoughts. I guess the reason I find this weird is that I've never felt this way about anyone, and all the things that my mind used to be able to ponder have been filled with moments Eric and I have spent together. As much as I enjoy it, it scares me. "Why not break it off with him just for a bit and try it out with Matt?" The words left me feeling so alone. I couldn't imagine doing that. I have a hard enough time going a weekend without him. I don't know what to say...it just feels weird even having the idea proposed.

People only know about me and my past if I choose to let them in. Those rare few that I do let in, who hear my stories continue to like me, I keep close and treasure. Those relationships are pure gold! There have only been three that I've told everything to: Joe, Alistair and Eric. How can I walk away from any of them?

16

Moving In together

This is the key from the first place Eric and I lived together. Holding the key in my hand I can feel the energy of our early love. *January 14th, 1998. Amanda announced the house will be sold when she graduates in April. Eric and I started talking about moving in together. It seems natural but scary. He is the only thing floating through my mind right now. We had an amazing night. There is something I have had running through my body all day. I wanted to say how important he is to me and how much I love him. I've been thinking*

about him a lot lately and enjoying the comfort of having him near. I love the idea of waking up every morning to him. I feel very special for having the chance to have such a relationship with someone whom I love so dearly.

I don't know what's going on right now, or why I feel so bad. I don't really understand what's happening. Perhaps I'm just not looking at the proper picture. I ask myself why I am bothered, but I know it's more than you simply saying that it's money. It's more than that. That much I know. Perhaps I'm just picking apart the last few weeks, but something is wrong. What really got me is that you said living with me was "impossible."

You said "You're not supposed to do that until your married."

"Is that why you don't want to live with me, because we've had sex already and there is nothing left?" I asked.

"I just have a lot of problems I'm thinking about." He ended the discussion.

Fine, is that what I am right now, a problem? I guess that's how I feel presently. I've spent most of my day thinking about us and I don't think I've accomplished anything. It's your choice. If you want to live with me, fine. If you want to go out with me, fine. If you just want to be friends, that's ok too. If you simply want me out of your life, I guess I'll be able to live with that also, because right now I know I don't feel good at all.

He went home for the weekend and called on Sunday. Now I feel even worse! He didn't even know I was bothered! At least he cleared up the previous issue. He said "I was mainly thinking about my money and not wanting to live with my roommates for another year."

"Great, that lifts some of this gray cloud, but my head still hurts all the same." I said.

He then made fun of me in front of his mom. I couldn't hear what he said, but his mom responded with "Is she pregnant? Is there a baby coming?"

He responded back saying, "At least not in the next year."

They were joking around at my expense? I didn't like that. "Whatever, I'm going to go." I said.

"I was just trying to defend myself." he said.

"Why do I need to be made fun of for you that? I'm just so frustrated. I give up. It's your choice. Continue or not." I hung up.

On Wednesday, April 22nd the Talking Psychic birthday calendar said: You're smart this year, but maybe a little reckless. You could get talked into an expensive deal by somebody you love, so take care regarding money in July. There may be almost too many opportunities to choose from in September. The one you choose may lead to a change in residence in the New Year. An inheritance or settlement comes through in November. Christmas bells could lead to wedding bells in February. Life will be more complete and less pressured in January. Devote your energies to family matters all month. You'll have high creative ideas in March. Rewards are around you, but you could be looking in the wrong place.

June 20th. Eric, know what? I love that I've got you in my life. Yeah, I'm getting sentimental, but it's true. I love living with you. I love being with you. I love knowing that you're here and I can wake you up if there is a bad phone call, or a scary dream, or I can call you on weekends when I miss you, knowing that you miss me too. I love getting little messages on the fridge and I love most of all waking up next to you in the morning and coming back to bed later on, to have you wake up to me.

I love the storms this August. The way trees glow, the energy in the air. Eric likes storms too; we often go out for walks in the rain. It is amazing to see something invisible like wind to have so much power. Today trees were coming down; we cleared a few large fallen branches from our street and then walked along the riverside. There was a shear wind coming straight at us. It took out two trees and a large branch was crackling right above us. Eric sheltered me and braced his arm, to avoid any blows as we ran to shelter. We waited out the worst of that storm in the washrooms with about ten other people caught in the rain. Then we continued our walk and got free cookies at Subway.

October 6th. I've been with Eric for a year and a half. Living together has been really nice for the most part. Today he sent me an email that sent butterflies fluttering everywhere. "I thought I would write you a quick note to tell you how much I care and how much I appreciated being woken up this morning. I don't think I have ever felt so warm and safe and comfortable as I do when I fall asleep with you beside me. I don't think I've ever felt so loved, as I do when I am in your arms. I don't think I'd have known all this, without you. Thank you for being there. Thank you for loving me."

October 24th 1998. I'm going to the big city for a conference, and Amanda asked if I'd be interested in going to a rave. I thought it would be fun. She told me that Keith and his friend were going to meet us, that we need tall guys for protection. She warned me that it might not be my scene.

Wow, it wasn't my scene, but still it was absolutely amazing. Standing room only, I was sandwiched with Keith behind me, the newbie, protecting me from unexpected body surfers. My body was moving to the music from the force of those who were surrounding me. The scene was absolutely amazing. We went back to Amanda's and crashed in her room.

May 1999. I don't know if I attract chaos and confusion, if I'm just in the right place at the right time or if I'm just a busybody, or maybe it's just another crazy spring. I looked out my window and saw smoke billowing from the neighbour's window. I ran out to see what was going on. I looked at her with her dog in her arms. Stunned, baffled and concerned all at once I asked "Where's the baby?"

She looked dazed as she stared at me "On the sofa." she told me.

I yelled to Eric, "Call 911; I'm going in."

I can't believe it; this lady rescued her dog and left her newborn lying on the sofa. The baby was still breathing. The fire was contained in the kitchen, so I was able to get out safely with the baby in my arms. I held on to her, not wanting to give her back to her mom, who had left her there to die. The little one was given about 20 minutes of oxygen from the fire-fighters when they showed, after which point I knew it was time to give her back.

A neighbour came up to me and commented "You ran into a burning house to save a baby? I'm not sure if that's brave or just stupid."

This forced a reflection on the value of life, the assessment of danger and risk. It clearly wasn't safe to go in, but my risk/gain evaluation knew it was the right thing to do. How could anyone not at least try?

This woman had family a few doors down the street and not even a month later there was another fire, in their house this time. *They came running down the street yelling "Fire!"*

I ran out asking "Where are the kids?"

"On the second floor." someone replied.

Eric asked "Does anyone have a ladder?" We went running to their house.

"Do you have a hose?" I asked, and noticed their neighbour did. I took their neighbour's garden hose to the curtains and couch at the front of the house – a candle by the window had ignited them when the wind brushed the curtain against the flame. Eric helped in the back with the ladder and kids. The kids got out safely and the fire was under control and smouldering when the fire-fighters arrived. It's crazy how intense brief moments of our lives can be. Today made me evaluate my priorities.

You never know how quickly things can change; I am going to get the most out of life! These two fire episodes were the start of my first-on-the-scene series. Maybe it was God giving me a quick introduction to the tasks and challenges planned for me.

Today is July 20th, 1999. Why is it so hard to let something you love so much go away? But I have to let you go, accept the job offer in the big city. It is your time to move on. Yet it feels so much like we are breaking up in my mind. You will no longer be with me, and I will no longer be able to get a hug when I need one. I have never loved anything as much as I love you. I guess that is why it hurts so much. I don't want to let you go and yet I know it is not my decision. If it was you would be here. You would stay here and we would leave together. I guess you leaving made me wonder about the instability of our relationship. I had to get up this morning because I couldn't stay in bed anymore. I wanted you gone already; the anticipation is so much worse. It's like I'm sitting here watching my life fall apart and there is nothing I can do to stop it. I wanted to leave this morning so badly, go out without saying good bye and not return until I knew you'd be gone. I want to punish you like I feel I am being punished. I guess that's the reason I don't want to talk to you. I know I'll break down. This is something I have to deal with. Being left by those I love. It's something I have a problem with.

We've talked a lot about the future; we've talked about getting married. But that's all it's been, talk! It's September and I just started a certificate program. I decided to push the topic and bought him a ring. The ring has been carved into this diary and locked away was because the evening was a great disappointment. Perhaps I wanted too much too soon. But I really believe that I am ready to move forward. We are living together. What else is there to married life?

He said he can't afford it currently. Well... I'm not asking for anything. I love him. I want to spend the rest of my life with him. I want it formal. Be he wouldn't even look at it.

I should have left it alone. But then I wouldn't have been happy. Am I happy now? I need more; the relationship has become stagnant. We are not "dating" anymore, just coexisting. I feel like I'm changing too much for something I want but am not getting.

It just seems like we are not going anywhere. He doesn't want to be dependent on me. I've never had anyone not accept a gift. He rejected my ring! Are we doomed? His rejection hurt me so badly. I put so much love, thought, and time into it... The least he could have done was look at it, try it on, and talk about how he's not ready for all that it holds... There are so many other ways he could have handled tonight.

Was this pay back? Is this how Nyles felt? Mark? Kzoo? Those relationships ended abruptly after I turned them down... Even Alistair and I stopped talking after that talk about marriage. Does that mean Eric and I will be over too? Sleeping alone in my bed, him in his room, never have I felt more unlovable.

Married Life 2000 to 2011

Deciding what I want out of life
and working towards that goal.

17

The Perfect Wedding

*I*t's December 1999. Four months and who knows how many fights later, it looks like he's staying. He was able to delay his acceptance of his job offer for six months and will start in June of 2000. He is finally feeling ready to announce an engagement. I've started my research. The best part was the party planning. I'm looking at small country inns. We are thinking about getting married somewhere central. I wanted a weekend wedding, no driving between locations, a full dinner, cocktails, drinks, dancing, and a DJ. The guys can have their cigars and *just walk a few short steps back to our rooms at the end of the night. I found a great place, almost the perfect location, very picturesque. This place has only 22 rooms, so the whole place will be ours, with no strangers. We can keep out anyone not in our current circle by simply saying there is not enough room. I prepared a weekend getaway for all. I wanted to pay for our guests' hotel rooms, dinners and breakfast. There would be no excuses for anyone invited not to come.*

The worst part about getting married was the drama that was involved. My mother wanted to invite family. Emily was my maid of honour, but for me that was enough. There are too many bad memories, too many secretes and too many stories I can't even mention because they are not mine to tell. It had taken me years of therapy to work through many of them. *I don't want "family" there on my wedding day. I want happy thoughts and love; it's my day. My mom doesn't understand the different effects our childhood had on all of us. I reflected on most of my childhood as what not to do, and moved my life in a different direction. Can I take back the invite?*

What? Now they think Jennifer is going to karaoke our first dance? I have had enough drama. Fine, she can sing and has a karaoke business; they are planning to provide DJ service. As nice as that is, I want to decline. This is my wedding, and my first dance. It has nothing to do with anyone else other than me and Eric. We are paying for it, so only our choices matter. If anyone doesn't like it, they don't have to come!!!

The only solution we came up with was to reduce the stress by not talking to our own families. Eric started talking to my family and I talked to his. We settled each other's battles to reduce our own emotional involvement. No one was going to ruin our wedding or our memories of it.

January 2000. I'm 23. *We went from planning for April 2001 to planning for one year earlier, and we will make our move to the big city as a married couple. We've chosen the weekend of our third anniversary for our wedding date. Mom is making the dresses; I've found some* pictures for mine and the bridesmaids' (Emily, Liz and Ursula who is one of Eric's good friends). The store didn't have a great selection of material. The one we picked wasn't the colour or pattern I wanted, but it was ok. I kept of piece of the dress material and added it to my memory tin.

It would be cool if we could have the ceremony outside; she's going to make me a velvet coat and capes for the girls. Eric is going to get a top hat and cane and his groomsmen (Joe, Darren, Keith) will have hankies that will match the girls' dresses, just to add some consistency in the photos. We want to use Becky's harpist, and she agreed to do it outside if it's not too cold. Eric and I kind of want snow. It always snows on April 6th, so maybe we'll luck out and get snow on the 8th too!

I coordinated the rooms and made a specialized basket for each guest, containing snacks, drinks and a gift to say thank you for sharing in our lives. There is also a room guide to find out where people are staying, name cards to hang from each door, processional cards and matching tissue packets for 'tears of joy' to go on their seats at the ceremony. The harpist was great, the room was perfect.

April 9th 2000. Yesterday, everything worked out as planned. (I'm removing my older sister, Eric's mom's attitude and the cigar from my memory.) It was everything we wanted, picturesque, and everyone kept telling us what a great idea it was to do everything at the inn. Almost everyone showed up on Friday night and joined us for dinner. It was great to see everyone! Saturday morning was filled with anticipation that unfolded perfectly. It started snowing just before the ceremony, so we had it inside, by the picture window. Eric and I walked in together, the tears of joy shared by all. Our eyes welled up with tears as we said "I do." The nondenominational pastor tried to lighten the mood by asking Eric "Is that your final answer?" It was a phrase from the television series Who Wants to be a Millionaire? We then took some pictures outside still with a light dusting of snow! We had cocktails and appetizers.

Dinner was great, combined with speeches. Terry, the detective from my dad's case, sent a letter to the inn. Darren was given it to read. He didn't know the extent of my relationship with Terry and the support he had been throughout my dad's investigation and trial. My mom told the group about Terry, how he came into our lives and how supportive he has been to us. Many of those at the wedding did not know the full story of the trial, and some knew nothing of the event, which added to the impact of the letter. Even after my dad's murder investigation and trial were over, Terry supported my interests and set up a ride along for me to go investigate some break-and-enters. He showed us his FBI pictures from Quantico. Even in university, he assisted when I wanted license plates run and talked me through any concerns I had. Then Darren read the letter.

> "*Memories of people we know often come into our lives unexpectedly. Often these people, although at first complete strangers, take their special place in our minds. Two of those people are as clear to me now as the first day we met. Today one became a bride. If I close my eyes, I can see Angela, and although I am not able to be present to see her, I am sure she is glowing with happiness.*
>
> *Several years ago I remember the first email from Angela telling me about her university experiences and the excitement of being away from home. Entering a new life was an exciting time, as it is today, when she starts on another journey. Although stressful, I am sure it was not as anxious for Angela as it was for Lana, who would worry about her girls so far from home. On the lighter side, I'm sure people had fewer busy signals when trying to phone their mother and that the phone company was also happy to free up some phone lines.*
>
> *Emails about university life told of studying and exams. Yes, there were reports of social activities, as is normal in university life, but Angela – rest assured those will remain in the deleted folder*

never to be accessed again. Your secrets are safe with me. Then – as is my prying nature, I would sneak in the odd "How's your love life?" question. Dead air was often the reply, but I was thrilled to finally learn of Eric and the life he and Angela were building. I knew it was serious when photographs of them began to appear on my screen – after those frustrating 30 minute downloads of course.

I was extremely pleased when I learned of today's wedding. Although I am not able to be there to see you smile or see the tears of joy, I want to wish you and Eric the best of lives together. And I want to tell you on a personal note that no matter how bad a day is, or what problems may arise, the best part of my day is just before I go to sleep when I hold my wife and tell her that I love her – because that fills me with life. And I truly wish you the same kind of happiness!

My love to you both on this special day.

Terry – the cop."

It was everything I wanted and more. All of the concerns about feeling empty, they were all gone. Terry somehow made all of that disappear. The evening went back to the present, being with each other and listening to all the other stories people had to say about us. The support, the love and the emotion were at a peak. I didn't want it to end and yet was really looking forward to some time in that Jacuzzi.

We said goodbye to most of our guests at breakfast on Sunday morning, then headed to the river and hung out a bit longer with a few of them. Part of it feels like goodbye, as we leave our friends and continue on to the big city. Eric's new position starts in June. We went to the city for some relaxation and started looking for our new home.

Almost as if my dreams knew a new chapter in my life had started, their intensity returned. They were no longer warning dreams, so much as messages to teach and heal. The first was in May of 2000, about Heaven and Hell.

I was at my Dad's house. There was a fight. I was trying to help out some friends and warn them of the attackers. I had my gun and was ready to fire. I stepped out of the bathroom into the hallway and just peeked around the corner. That's when I felt a sharp pain rip through my side. I collapsed in pain; Thalia (a friend from school) attempted to bring me back in to the safety of the bathroom.

Once in there, I told her "I am ready to go, but I need your help. Finish me off, please."

"I can't do it," she said, "but I don't want to see you in so much pain either." We cried in each other's arms.

"I don't have much time," I told her "I need to talk to my mother." She was in my dad's bedroom.

Struggling to the hallway so I could see her, my mom told me "If you see three hills, you are going to heaven and I will follow you soon. I pray they aren't mountains, because I really miss you."

With that I voyaged into the living room. I could feel each bullet enter me with a warm welcome. There was no more pain. It didn't hurt anymore.

For a moment all was black, then my surroundings disappeared and I saw the hills, but there were four of them. I had to tell my mother there were four, not three. I began to move, but the shell of my body remained on the floor. The man who had shot me was inspecting his work. I raised my old body's arm and sent him running.

I told my mother, "There are four hills not three."

"It'll be ok." she assured me. She hugged me and I flew towards the hills.

I arrived at what appeared to be a city. There were houses lined at the base of the hill, continuing up the slope. It looked like such a pretty town. I began to investigate. As I was walking, I saw very few people, but stopped to observe a squirrel when a young man asked me, "Do you need any help?"

"No, I'm ok thanks." I responded.

"You look new here." I turned to see this beautiful man in a relaxed fitted white suit.

"I don't know what to ask. I don't know what there is, so I have no point of reference to start from." I responded.

He smiled and informed me there was a meeting shortly and I should probably attend. We talked as we walked to the meeting. He introduced himself as "John."

"What is it like here?" I asked.

"It is whatever you make of it." he told me. "You'll learn more at the meeting."

We arrived at a large outdoor banquet area, with about 300 people all around my age. John introduced himself to the group, welcomed us all, and began answering my question.

"There are many things that you can do in Heaven. There are a variety of levels you can aspire to and work towards. Heaven becomes whatever you want it to be. There were four levels. In the first you do what you choose, you explore, learn about your surroundings and space. You enjoy the weather and meet old friends.

The second level requires some studies; you learn about history, people, and spirituality. It allows you to become more aware of your surroundings. The third is a continuation of the studies to include all sentient beings and knowledge of how everything fits into one working system. The fourth is an awareness of yourself and the universe, realization of what needs to be changed and what one person can do. Upon completion of the fourth level, you can choose to return to Earth to accomplish your realization. You will each have a guide."

The meeting was done, and John was beside me again, "You've done that a few times." he told me. It all seemed familiar. I had a task, and I returned to Earth with a purpose.

"There is a list of all those who've joined us over the years. It has their name, photo and current stage or level." he informed me. "Are you sure you are ready for that list?" he asked me.

"Yes" I replied as if not looking was never an option.

"Are you prepared to see what you find?" he asked.

I searched the list for 1992, and at the end of November I just started scanning the faces. "Where is he?" I was becoming frantic.

"Angela, it's ok." John tried to console me.

"Where is his photo?" I demanded.

"Angela, your father has never joined us." he told me.

"I don't understand." I started.

"Do you think he deserved to?" His words were obvious as soon as they were spoken.

"Where else do people go?" I inquired solemnly.

John looked at me as if questioning whether I was ready for this. "Let's walk." he said as he put his arm around me. "All spirits that don't come here have the chance to regain themselves. They are allowed to send mind messages to all those whom they harmed. It is required that those they hurt are understanding, and if they can get them to work through any problems that may remain, if the victims are willing to forgive, then the spirit can progress to heaven. If not, they stay in the study room."

"What is the study room like?" I asked cautiously, curious.

"It is a one-dimensional area, almost like they don't exist. But in losing their bodies, they were left with three heightened senses. They have the ability to hear your thoughts, see your pain, (touch and taste have been taken away) and for conditioning purposes there is a permanent odour (the smell of death) to remind them continuously of all the wrong they have done." he told me.

We kept walking. He showed me to my house. I entered and decided to have a rest on the big couch. I fell asleep, which is when I woke up.

I think that is why it took me so long to forgive my dad. Talking to him in my head often helped. *"It hurt me when you never gave me a hug that last weekend we saw you. It was the last time we saw you alive and you were so cold. I wanted you to love me so badly, but all you could do was hurt me and then try and pay for it with purchases. You couldn't show love and that's what I needed. I internalized you not loving me as me being unlovable. I wanted to show you that you could love me. I wanted to show you that I could be loved and that I could love. You never signed a single card with "Love, Dad." It was always just "Dad." I know I will never have the chance to have you love me, but I still have time to forgive you and love you."*

I had to come to terms with the fact that he did the best he could with what he had. I just wish I had the chance to see him change. I believe he could have become a better person and I could have developed an adult relationship with him. I would have loved to discuss my childhood with him, to figure out where his mind was. I'm certain he was a better father than his father was! Shortly after I forgave my father, I awoke from a long-desired dream, the tears streaming down my face. My Dad gave me the gift I've always wanted.

Somehow the dream took care of everything. Finally, I had a moment of peace in which I could feel loved. I got my final hug and the warm fuzzy feelings of knowing I meant something to someone else. The dream helped by giving me a reward for all the work I had done in the effort to forgive. It was the best gift he could have given me.

The Gift

The other night I had a dream: you came to visit me.
You saw me now, all grown up; you said I made you proud.
But you said there was something I was missing.
You took me on a trip to Australia; you said I've always wanted.
We went scuba diving in the waters and took a long walk
along the shores.

We ended on the pier looking out at the vastness.

You put your arm around me; you said you had to go.

But this time, you said, you wanted to leave me with a happy memory.

Angela, 2000

July 2000, I had another significant dream which I titled "Waking Up."

There was a bad mind controller and he wanted to be my boyfriend. We were in his house; I was moving in. We had some friends over and as I showed them the house I told them, "This is where I go when I dream."

Inside the room there were four people. One was a machine controller who was angrily dropping small gold CDs onto my chest, and they would simply be absorbed. I was scared, and as the series of CDs was about to be dropped by this mechanical arm, a force pulled me off of the table and I landed where an old man was. I knew the CDs were my memories and new memories they were trying to impose on me. I managed to escape unseen.

In the next room there were a bunch of tables and the good mind controller was in there. He complimented my change in hairstyle and colour. It was my attempt to be myself and escape the controls of others. He knew what the bad mind controller was trying to do. The good mind controller started talking with a magician.

Suddenly I was in the audience of the theatre; there were thousands of people in the audience. On the ground there was a big picture, as if there was a camera on the magician and his image was being projected on the ground.

The bad mind controller entered the room and got into an argument with the good mind controller. I knew we needed to get everyone out. While the good mind controller kept the bad mind controller busy, I helped everyone get away. It seemed almost like we were exiting a ship. We had been trapped and brainwashed to believe if we left, the outside elements would kill us.

The air outside was unexpectedly breathable; I looked up and the sky was blue and sunny.

Eric moved and I woke up. I told him the dream. It felt like the place was being destroyed because of these mind controllers, and when I freed all the people we broke the hold they had on our minds.

"They are still here." I told Eric.

"Others are remembering what happened." the voice said.

Suddenly I was in tears, overcome with sadness. It wasn't a sadness I felt, but rather one being forced upon me. I could hear the voices. They were arguing with each other.

"We need her." the first voice said.

"She's not ready." said the second voice.

I was breathless. I felt the energy of the first voice was trying to take me away to another dimension, while the energy of the second voice was holding me in place.

I reached over and grabbed Eric. He saw me struggling to breathe. I screamed in my head: "This is where I am. This is where I want to be!" Slowly the air returned to my lungs.

I could hear the first voice saying "This life isn't anything. This isn't where you are supposed to be." There was a strong urgency in this statement, as though the voice was convinced I was supposed to let go of this life.

The voices continued to argue. "Can't you see what you're doing to her? She's not ready." voice two said.

"But we need her now. It can't wait any longer." Then, it seemed almost like they stopped arguing to see what I was doing, and they realized I was conveying everything to Eric and he was writing it down.

"They are doing a memory wipe." I said. I could feel them erasing my dream, my memory of the thoughts: it was all gone.

I could hear a voice say "You're not supposed to remember this."

Eric had written it all down. I looked at him, stunned. "What's going on?" I asked.

"You had an intense dream; I wrote it down." He started to read it back to me. It was only a vague memory in my mind. I read it over and over and over to slowly piece back together the dream, the faces, the events...

The dream held the intensity that it did because of the continuation after I awoke. Eric beside me filled me with love and purpose, reasons to hold on to what I had and where I was.

18

Finding a Job

*I*n small towns buses came every 20 minutes if you were lucky, so I often used my bike for transportation. The first time I needed the subway, I asked my friend what the schedule was and was baffled to learn it was only three to five minutes between trains. Suddenly the big city didn't seem so big. I kept a token from my days of interviews and trips all over the city looking for a job.

My first job related to my professional field was providing respite care. I worked with families in their homes providing care and following through on their therapy plans. I would help with hygiene, nutrition, exercise, and recreational activities. I would try to improve quality of life while working on self-help skills. I was with this one family for almost a year. When I started working with them, my client would sit there and self-stimulate by flapping her hands and poking herself in the eye. I managed to teach her how to crawl, use ten words in American Sign Language, and had her very close to being toilet trained. It was very rewarding to see her progress, but I was emotionally challenged by the job.

The underlying problem was that I started noticing things during diaper changes that were clearly not normal. Her anus began to relax and widen, and stopped being fully closed after a bowel movement. Every time I changed her diaper, my memories of childhood returned. I needed to save her, to stop the abuse and its effects. *I told my supervisor my concerns about the dad abusing his daughter. She told me that over 80% of children with special needs are abused. I told her that didn't make it ok. Suddenly I was deflated. All of my experiences dismissed all of my pain seemingly acceptable because of the statistics? She wasn't going to report it. The laws need to change!* (They did just a few years later – now everyone has a duty to report suspected child abuse.)

This morning the dad asked me "What do you wear to sleep?" I knew I had to quit. He had been flirtatious before and I'd always rejected it.

"That is completely inappropriate." I responded.

I went to tell the mom "I can't work here anymore, your husband has continued to make unwanted passes at me and I've asked him to stop."

Her only response was "Oh, no. Not again."

January 2ⁿᵈ 2001 I loved my new job until today. I work in an infant room and weekend recreation centre. I devise recreation programs for children. I get to play. It is so much better than my last position. The problem was I got attached to the infants in my care. I got attached to their families and I had a really hard time when they died.

Life and Death

I understand that all life must end.

I understand that his time had come.

I realize the difference, celebrating life and mourning death.

But what life there was to celebrate?

17/07/98 - 31/12/00.

How long is that?

A lifetime, evidently.

A lifetime of hospitals, surgery, and inconsistencies.

What kind of a life is that?

His life evidently.

Two deaths now.

It's too many.

Angela, 2000

March 21st 2001. *One of my favourite little ones came back from the Intensive Care Unit for the third time and now had a Do Not Resuscitate order. I was floored. She came to program quieter than usual. Her mom was with her, as always. We were doing a sensory activity with the children, and her mom in a chair rocking her when and she arrested. Her little heart stopped beating. Her mother rocked her back and forth in the rocking chair. "It's alright, it's alright, it's alright." she repeated, seemingly trying to convince herself it would be ok. Tears started streaming down her face, and mine. There was nothing I could do. One of the little ones I had allowed myself to get so close to was dying, dead, her little body was lifeless before me. I was done. I am done.*

August 2001. I applied to work at a childcare centre and got a position as lead for the infant room and the therapeutic play room, as well as acting supervisor in her absence. I've been here a week and today was my first day replacing the supervisor. I don't know where she had to go, but as second in command, I took over. Things were going fine for the first 20 minutes or so, but then crazy took over.

Gunshots filled the air. We could hear them. I got a call from the supervisor at a neighbouring centre confirming that I was to put the centre under lockdown. What that means is that all curtains must be closed, all doors locked and all the kids have to go into the hallway, away from doors and windows. Kids were freaking out, and the teachers were freaking out. I had to keep everyone calm, deal with parents' phone calls and concerns, and conduct a perimeter check. I had to check each and every room, closet, and cupboard to ensure the gunman was not inside our building! Once I confirmed our building was safe and in lockdown, I needed to await police clearance before I could let any parents inside to get their kids. What a day! Home now, with a glass of wine, it's time to update the resume again.

Well, I got it! They reduced four postings to just two and I got it. It's a brand new program they are developing. I'll get trained by these specialists and develop the framework for this new program. I'll help establish policies and procedures, have meetings with the community, locate and negotiate clinic space, and provide training to a variety of health care professionals. I'm so thrilled! I'm finally out of childcare and feeling so professional. It felt amazing to walk into that office, head held, high feeling like I finally made it!

19

A House and Kids

*A*ugust 2002. We managed to pay off our student loans and saved up enough for a down payment. We started looking for a house. We found our area, looked at the zoning and found a quiet little corner neighbourhood just off the highway and near a major street. Houses in our price range were really bizarre. *Today we went to see two houses that were ridiculous. The first claimed to have a partially finished basement. The basement consisted of a dirt floor, sloping up to the base of the external walls of the house. At the*

base of the stairs there was a furnace and a rocking chair. It just looked creepy. The second house mentioned one and a half bathrooms. It was ok for the most part, except for the small linen closet that was converted to a room with a toilet, and the sink was hidden in the desk in the second bedroom! We kept looking and told our real estate agent that we might consider raising our maximum price limit.

October 2002. We pulled up to two houses side by side, both for sale. "This is it." I told Eric.

"No, it's number five." he responded.

"I can see you teaching a young boy to ride a bike on the green path behind the house. I'm inside. It's number seven."

The real estate agent told us that although number seven was also for sale, it was $125,000 over our limit. We looked at number five. It was perfect, so we put in an offer. The bank said we could do it. This house backed on to a green path with shopping and schools close by. There was also a major intersection within a ten minute walk. Another bidder put in an offer at the same time and we maxed out our bid. Evidently, the other bidder outbid us. We were deflated, but the hunt was back on.

The next week we got a call saying number seven lowered the price. We went to visit this house and found it covered in wall paper, even the ceilings. There were new windows, a new furnace and a new roof, but pink flowery wall paper everywhere! I knew this was meant to be ours. I took a small grey rock from the flowerbed. We put in our offer and it went back and forth twice before she finally accepted the same price as next door. Eric and I were the proud new owners of pink flowery wallpaper! We moved in, and room by room made it our home.

May 2003. Eric and I met up at our favourite restaurant. It was the quiet corner that was our meeting place. We talked and talked and talked. We had completed our five year plan in just three years. It seemed like it was time to consider the next five years. We agreed it included a little one. We are planning for Feb 29th, 2004 as our due date. It was the best sex ever:

making love with the intent to create life was mind blowing, and we did everything we could to make it the most memorable. One of my favourites is the breathless kiss Alistair described once. When combined with sex, the rhythm adds so much more. Eventually, one of us needs a fresh breath of air, turning everything into a passionate moment of kissing.

Disappointed that it didn't work, I got concerned and made an appointment with my doctor. I asked "Why didn't I get pregnant?"

She asked that embarrassing question; "Are you doing it right?"

Baffled, not knowing there was a wrong way, I described what we did.

She told us, "It takes about 36-48 hours to replenish a healthy sperm supply, so you need to slow down." It took us two months to conceive.

August 14th, 2003. Wow, that was perfect timing, and what a memorable day. I took the test this morning, and it came back positive. I thought I'd go and get Eric a "congratulations, you are going to be a dad!" gift, a last bottle of wine (if I can't drink, he won't be drinking either) and dinner. I left work an hour early and went to the mall to pick up an addition to a simple coin collection that would one day be passed on. I filled up the gas tank, picked up the wine and groceries and went home to prepare. I pulled into the driveway and heard honking. I looked around to notice the lights at the end of the street had gone out.

Eric called my cell. "Is the power out at home?" he asked.

I went inside and found that it was. "Yup, we are without power." I told him.

He was downtown. I turned on the back up radio to learn that it was a city-wide outage. Eric was going to catch a ride home with a friend. The radio then slowly informed us of how widespread the outage was, throughout the North-Eastern US and Ontario, with 55 million people affected.

After his lengthy voyage home, Eric and I enjoyed our dinner celebrating our life and the changes to come. With no work Friday, we partied the rest of the weekend to use up the perishable food. We invited over our friends who lived in condos (no elevators or water) and barbecued *all weekend. Being a survivalist pays off: we had all the supplies needed to only be affected by cold showers on day three. Monday, work was still cancelled; most of the city was still without power, so it was a great long weekend to welcome our new test results!*

It's been quite a life change, improving my nutrition, sleeping and exercising, but being pregnant is easier than I thought. I haven't had any nausea, and no other real changes other than the lack of monthly cycles. I really miss wine and chocolate martinis. Today was the first time I really felt pregnant. The little one kick me today for the first time! Every movement was such a thrill. This little person, part-me part-Eric was growing inside me. When we heard his heart beat for the first time, we called home to let the voicemail record it. We kept that on our phone for over three years!

We had a name picked out quickly: Caitlyn Celeste. We both liked it, but the ultrasound came back indicating the little one inside me was a boy. We were playing with a few names but decided to go with patterns. The first name would start with an "E" (for Eric) and end in an "an" (for Angela). The middle name would be reversed; "A" (for Angela) and "er" (for Eric). So, we ended up with Ethan Alexander.

Eric and I were thrilled when the first contractions became regular. Emily and Mom happened to be stopping by that evening after a show. We were excited to share the news and they both stayed. By three in the morning I could no longer sleep through the contractions, as they were intensifying, and by seven in the morning they had been five minutes apart for an hour, so we called Christine, our midwife. She came over and checked me out. Everything slowed down. I was only 2cm dilated and contractions slowed back down to every 20 minutes.

My birth plan had us going out for our last meal with the early labour, to calm, distract and have a drink (I was now allowed). Mom thought that was a bad idea and we ended up not going. It was late evening Saturday when contractions were back to the five minute mark. Christine came back with her carload of supplies, but everything slowed down again...The plan was still to birth at home, so she kept monitoring his movements, his heart rate, my heart rate and my blood pressure. We were both coping well. Sunday morning she had me going up and down the stairs, and in the shower, but nothing could get me over that 3cm mark. By seven Sunday evening, I had enough. We wanted this little guy out. She ruptured my membrane and we headed in to the hospital for some drugs. I needed a nap.

I hated the anaesthesiologist. Eric got into a fight with him while I was in the middle of a contraction. This guy wanted to shove a needle in my back that could paralyze me if I moved. Eric wanted him to wait one minute for this contraction to end. My mom started arguing with Eric for arguing with the anaesthesiologist. It was a mess. Finally, the pain was gone and I went to sleep. I woke up around three in the morning, fully dilated and ready to push. Christine asked me to try one push just to monitor movement and then quickly told me to stop; she needed to call the other midwife. "This baby is coming out." He didn't tuck his head properly, and gave me back labour and a second degree tear on my cervix, but somehow managed to make it out. It was 5:45am, April 26th, 2004, when Ethan entered our world. The cord was around his neck with a true knot in it. It didn't matter that he was covered in his gooey amniotic fluid. Eric and I were instantly in tears. Intense feelings of immediate love for a little person flooded over us like a wave sucking us in. He was beautiful. His little body grown inside me, of Eric's seed, parts of both of us, combined in love. It was amazing.

Ethan's cord was confirmed as having only two vessels: one vein, one artery. We were going to have to get him an ultrasound and some testing. His kidneys turned out fine, and everything looked normal. But we were placed on high alert for bladder infections and told to go straight to the Emergency Room if there was ever any concern.

The euphoria gave way to sleep deprivation and four months of post-partum tears and hormonal ups and downs. When Eric returned to work, isolation kicked in. My network, my supports, my friends all continued their day jobs. I was stuck at home with this little person fully dependent *on me, seemingly unable to stop his inconsolable screaming. These were the longest months of my life. He would only sleep on me, and if I put him down he'd wake up and the screaming would start again. So after bathing, changing, nursing and walking, if I was lucky he'd fall asleep and I was stuck. He woke up if I sat down, he woke up if I stopped moving, and those people who told me to sleep when he slept clearly didn't have the same situation. One of the few moments of solace I got was with an elderly neighbour, Merle. She had low vision and early stages of Alzheimer's but these two seemed to need each other. During some of his inconsolable moments, I'd go and knock on her door. "Who is it?" she'd always ask.*

"Angela." I'd say. It seemed like a dance sometimes.

"Who?" she'd repeat.

"Angela." I'd respond, but she never remembered me. I'd have to hold Ethan up to the window and instantly she'd remember.

"Oh, Ethan, come on in." She remembered him. He would stop crying and she'd start telling me stories about her children. It was almost like they needed each other.

One day he was crying inconsolably, Merle had been moved to a medical care centre and I did everything I could, then to prevent my own tears I left him on the main floor and went upstairs just to go to the bathroom… one minute of peace. But things went silent. He went quiet and I was instantly concerned. I remembered the moment when my favourite child from the rehabilitation centre when quiet. So many things can go wrong. I rushed downstairs to find him sleeping in the Moses basket right where I left him. He was sleeping on his own! I had my first break in months. I had a nap.

June 30th, 2004. I got a letter stating that the guy imprisoned for the murder of my father had waived his right to a parole hearing. Now, at home with a two-month-old infant and a nasty case of post-partum depression, it hit me hard. It said "Please note that I am unable to share with you the reasons for his decision to waive the hearing. He remains in custody."

What does that mean? Is he afraid? Maybe he didn't do it and the real killer had said "If you leave or talk, I'll get you!" Maybe I'm still in danger too. I can't believe my mom gave my siblings my contact info when I was pregnant. I'm so glad I changed my number.

The letter said "A hearing has been scheduled for November 2006 in relation to the full parole review date that has been set for December 15, 2006." Should I go to the parole hearing? How do I disguise myself? Could I change my weight, or wear a wig? Can I hire a private detective to attend, record it and let me know what happened? Could they tell me who was there and how he looked. I started calling private investigators, but the next hearing was over two years away.

I often got freaked out by my life and slowed down with the spirituality stuff. Then, dreams would slowly draw me back into the surreal experiences. I had constant reminders and moments that my spiritual journey was being forced on me. At times, I would accept the moments, but at times I would run from them. *In November 2004, I felt it was time to learn more about what is going on. A college catalogue came in the mail; I noticed they had a certificate program for holistic healing. There were a few weird coincidences with a colleague, Josée, so I said I'd sign up if she did. One day we had a guest speaker. At break, he came up to me and commented, "You have some baggage."*

"Hmm. Really? Me? Baggage?" I responded, half laughing at him. You don't need to be intuitive to pick up on my baggage.

"Can I use you for an example?" he asked.

"Sure, my life's an open book." I responded.

He set up two chairs facing each other. "Look into my eyes. What do you see?"

Suddenly his face morphed into my dad's. "I see my dad." I was trembling, feeling like that scared child once more. Then, almost as if I was in an automatic trance...he was in my head. His eyes began to water.

"Did he hurt you?" he asked.

"Yes." I responded.

"Emotionally?" he continued.

"Yes." I said.

"Physically?" he asked. The questions and answers flowed as I stared into my dad's eyes, safe, knowing he was dead, and I was in the classroom. He couldn't hurt me anymore, so I was safe to respond.

"Yes." I said.

"Sexually?" he asked.

"Yes." I said.

The words poured out of my mouth before I had a chance to think or filter. Tears welled up in my eyes. I could feel the supportive energy pouring in from Josée and the class.

I wiped away tears and refocused on the guest speaker. He asked "What do you need to say?"

"I deserved better." I said. The tears began a free flow as I said what I needed to say. "You were supposed to be my dad, provide support and encouragement, but you didn't. You stole my childhood, scarred me for life and all I ever wanted was to feel loved. Now you are the one who has lost out. You never got to know me, or see me grow up. I made it."

The anger and the hate were melting away. Slowly I became present in the classroom, aware of my surroundings; I noticed ever single classmate was in tears. He gave me his card, in case I had anything else I needed to finish up.

I was curious how much baggage I still had and called him to continue therapy. He liked to use meditation in his sessions. I could feel him inside my brain going through bookshelves of memories, and he could zone in on a specific memory. It was like he opened a book and I knew what we needed to talk about. It was amazing to have a therapist who used his empathy skills to read me and figure out which issues I still needed to work on.

During therapy with the empath there were discussions of my father and another abuser from childhood molesting me. Therapy with the empath was bizarre because his face would morph into the face of my abuser and I knew what needed to be said. He would also ask questions, sometimes in such a way that automatic responses escaped my mouth seemingly in a mild hypnosis, often pulling at things from long ago that I didn't have in my conscious memories.

Things got progressively supernatural. One day my teacher was talking about working with Reiki energy. As she spoke, I began to see energy around her. This was the first time that the energy around someone had taken on colour; it was a yellowish orange. I was now seeing people's auras.

I hadn't had any experiences like that since the voices during my pregnancy. One day, I was driving a voice spoke.

"Switch lanes." it told me.

"But I'm taking the next exit." I verbally responded.

"Switch lanes!" it demanded.

"It doesn't make sense." I argued back.

"Now!" it yelled.

"Fine!" I did.

Then it happened: a three car pileup. I could have been in the middle of it and likely dead. I pulled over. The extra car space I provided by moving was enough of a buffer and there were no life threatening injuries. The voices often gave me directions when driving. During those nine months, I was first on scene for about five car accidents, making the 911 calls and providing basic first aid until EMS arrived.

There is something going on with Ethan. We were interviewing home daycares, and what took me 20 minutes to figure out he knew in seconds. *We walked into this one home and he started screaming. As I tried to calm him, she proceeded to show me her place.*

"And this is where I change their little bums." she said patted her bed.

My first thought was "Where are the others while you take one into your bedroom?"

We went into the living room to see a big chest freezer behind the sofa. "Thank you." I said finally understanding what my eight-month-old was trying to tell me, and we left.

June 2005, I took a course on dreams. It was an amazing class. Wendy from the holistic class was also taking the dreams course. She and I seemed to have an interesting connection. We were talking about dream sharing; our teacher was referring to writing down dreams and discussing them. I asked about connecting within dreams. She said it was rare, but with my dreaming abilities, she thought it might be possible. Wendy and I decided to try one night after class. The plan was that we would journal about meeting up in the dream world and bring our notes to the next class.

Wow. Wendy and I had almost the same journal entries. We both described the clothes, dialogue, the Viking ship, and the waterfall. They were so similar it was a bit freaky.

October 2005. I signed up for a Reiki class. Wendy and I were partners. I learned about focusing energy, guarding myself and shaking off bad energy. The classes came in handy when it came to bumps and bruises with my kids. One day, Ethan had a nasty fall. As I ran for the ice I called out to Wendy, Josée and my teacher in my head: "Help me, I need your energy!" I sat with Ethan on my lap, his goose egg so big the skin was about to break. He screamed when I put ice on it. I tried Reiki. "Please God, help me." Slowly, I could see it disappearing. I held my hand in place, breathing slowly, allowing distance healing to assist; he stopped crying and asked for an ice cream. By the time Eric got home, it was just a small bruise.

In June 22nd 2006, I got another piece of mail indicating the guy in prison for killing my dad had waived his right to parole again. It bothered me a bit, but I've been thinking... either he did it and he's not rehabilitating and it's good for him to stay in prison, or he didn't do it and he's afraid to leave. Either way, as long as he is behind bars, my world remains constant. In addition to the letters that he has waived his parole, I started getting phone calls that he was being relocated and that he was being granted temporary absences for medical purposes. Over the next years he was relocated again and again and waved his right to parole again and again. I stopped keeping track. So what will happen... he'll reach 25 years in 2017, and then what? Do they just let him out, sentence served?

Making the decision to have a second child was a very slow process. We realized Ethan would never know a cousin. Emily had offered her husband Mark, 80 grand for a car instead of kids; she said it would be easier and cheaper. Ethan needed to have someone to complain about his parents to. It's a big responsibility to be the end of the line for the family and we thought he needed someone to share that with. We still had that name, Caitlyn Celeste, another spirit that seems to be waiting for us. Eric's siblings, Heather and Joe, didn't look like they were going to have kids. Ethan was almost three years old when we started missing the new-abilities-every-day baby stage and decided to go ahead. We thought Halloween would be a good due date and fully lined up for it, but again it took us two months. It looked like this one would be a Christmas baby. Maybe our kids are just destined to be born near to our own birthdays.

February 2nd, 2007. *Best compliment ever! Martyn, an expert in the field, was endless in his compliments this morning at the conference I organized. I directed the slides of his presentation and he used my stats to discuss variety in individuals' abilities, naming and highlighting me as the best. Furthermore, he publically thanked me for some data I initiated and provided. He published it and presented it internationally last month! It was an amazing morning! He told everyone my research will be used as an international benchmark.*

In May 2007, things got intense again. *I'm not sure how to deal with Ethan sometimes. He is very perceptive. He knows things and sees things that I can't see. We were driving to the store today and he burst into tears.*

"What's wrong?" I asked him.

Through sobs, he pointed and said "I hate those people!"

There was a couple walking down the street. "What happened?" I asked, bewildered.

"They hurt their son!" he continued through his tears.

"I don't see a boy with them." I commented.

"Not anymore!" he said, hardly audible as tears took over.

I tried to talk to him about his perceptions. He could read people from early on. Maybe it has something to do with heightened sensitivity for all of us during my pregnancy. I wonder if his tears as an infant had any correlation to his perception of my post partum blues.

Lying in bed I couldn't sleep, and a white light silhouette of a woman came into the room. I did the protective energy bubble that pushes away all negative energy, but she remained.

She was light and beautiful. I asked "Who are you and why are you here?"

"My name is Martha." she told me. "I'm here to help keep Ethan safe."

There was an image of Ethan being wrapped in a silk-like material that put him in a bubble of safety. Next, I could see the house from above. My protective bubble appeared weak. She put her hands over mine to strengthen the shield of protection.

"This will do for now." she said, and the light faded and I was back in bed.

A few nights later, I woke up to Ethan making noises. I went into his room and he seemed to be talking.

"... illy" I heard him say.

"Billy?" I asked.

"Emily." he corrected me.

"Are you ok?" I asked.

"Yes, can I have more music please?" He asked in a sleepy state. I reset his music timer, and he snuggled up on me and went back to sleep. I returned to my bed.

His music stopped so I went back in and saw a dark shadow by his bed. I tried to zap it out with a protective energy but it remained. I repeated my attempt, but still it remained.

"Leave!" I told it.

"I'm here to protect Ethan." it told me.

"Who are you?" I demanded.

"Michael, the archangel." he said.

"If you are an angel, prove it!" I insisted, not willing to tolerate just any spirit at my son's bedside. I knew nothing of angels or what an archangel was or who Michael was.

Without a word, Michael stood up. He was suddenly brilliant bluish silvery light and his wingspan filled the room. It was an amazing sight to behold.

"If you are an angel, why are you dark and crouching?" I asked.

"When I come in my true form, Ethan wakes and stops talking." he said.

"Why are you here?" I questioned.

"I am the angel of keeping children healthy and safe." he explained further.

"But Ethan is coughing." I said doubting his skill.

"I can fix that." he told me. I counted in my head slowly to 30, and there were no more coughs.

"Why does Ethan get an archangel? What about all the other children who need you?" Images of the little ones from the children's hospital came to mind.

"It is his destiny." he told me "Ethan is mean to do great things."

"You can stay." I told him.

Michael stayed by Ethan's bedside in his blue form but now crouching again on the floor. I returned to my room and Eric awoke.

"Do you know anything about Archangel Michael?" I asked Eric.

"He is a messenger, the voice of God and protector of children."

"He is in Ethan's room right now." I told him about our encounter. Slowly, I felt a warm blanket covering me in layers of peaceful protection, and camouflage engulfed my home. I fell into a deep restful sleep.

Michael and Martha weren't the only spirits to visit Ethan. On May 27th, Ethan awoke from a nap and looked like he was having a seizure.

"Look at me." I told him.

He did, and then returned to looking at the corner of the ceiling.

"What do you see?" I asked.

"Ball." he told me.

"What colour is it?" I probed further.

"Red." he responded.

"Is it scary?" I asked.

"No." he told me.

"Do you want it to go away?" I asked, trying to find out more about what he felt.

"No." he again responded.

But then, he had another seizure-like bodily response. "Ethan, it needs to leave."

I envisioned a cleansing and protective bubble around Ethan enlarging to fill the room, pushing all entities out. I then enlarged it to the entire house.

"Is it gone?" I asked.

"No." Ethan responded.

"Ethan, you need to tell it to go away. Leave now!" I said, strengthening the protection bubble and for a second time pushing all entities out of my home.

"It's gone." Ethan said his eyes now able to re-focus on mine.

June 10ᵗʰ, 2007. Round two of pregnancy has been completely different. The fifth or sixth week, the nausea started. Week 12 I needed a new pant size. With Ethan, I was almost seven months in before I needed the next size. But today was more that I could handle. Ang and Dave lost theirs. They were 12 weeks, and we were going to be delivering within a few weeks of each other, on maternity leave together. It was going to be great and now it's gone. She felt something was wrong, went in for her check-up and was told. It sucked.

Ok, that was just mean. I had a dream the other night: Caitlyn said she wanted to bring a friend with her. Today, when Christine was using the Doppler to let us hear the heartbeat, for the first time there seemed to be multiples.

"There it is." she told us, and then it moved.

"Oh, there it is." she said, seemingly finding the heart beat again.

"There might be more than one in there, "she said.

Ok, that wasn't encouraging. We went to get an ultrasound… that technician sounded a lot like Christine.

"There's the head, oh, wait, there's the head." she started. "Um, are you having multiples?" she asked.

WHAT? Isn't she the one who is supposed to be clarifying that? She had to get the doctor, he took over the ultrasound. "Nope, just one in there and it's a boy!"

August 29th, 2007 we were at an amusement park. I had completed only 23 weeks of my 40 week gestation. I felt cramps and moisture. I went to the washroom to find blood, and instantly the cramps intensified in my state of shock. All I could think of was Ang and Dave, and all those who we've known who miscarried. I called Christine.

"Sit tight," she told me, "I'll come check you out."

"We are at an amusement park out of town." I told her.

"Relax for a moment, but then it's time to come home." she instructed.

She met us at our place. The baby's heart rate was ok; things were ok, except me. I was not ok. 23 weeks meant viability was next week! This sucks. But the bleeding and contractions stopped. Everything is fine again. My mind is such a mess.

At 25 weeks, the bleeding and contractions started up again. It was the same thing, and this time she had me meet her at the hospital. I can't take this. He'd only weigh one and a half pounds, if I'm lucky. Celestol? Is that really required? They came at me with a needle. What did they just say? It was to give his lungs a chance? I'm not ready. It's too early. Can't you stop it? Just sew me shut? God, can't you stop it? Wendy, Josée send me Reiki or something! Don't let him out this early! He would be so tiny, with so many complications. Christine told me my cervix is dilating, but the contractions are not regular. They even gave me a second shot 12 hours later, just in case!

Bed rest sucks! At least he stayed in. I'm off work, and need three days without contractions or bleeding. I'm going crazy! To distract myself I got a vendor permit and started a toy store. It gives me something to focus on, *a mental distraction. We buy so many toys anyways, so we might as well get them at cost. I need to at least make it to 27 weeks. I'd prefer 32, but anything would be better than 25. My brain is complete mush. My tears are never-ending. My connection with God is pleading.*

I made it. After two weeks of rest I'm at 27 weeks of gestation. The little guy might be over two pounds. The contractions have not stopped, but the bleeding has. I made it back to work with office duties only, no lifting, no walking. I could only sit and it was suggested my feet be up and resting. I was surrounded by nurses, so what could go wrong. Every time I had an intense contraction, the nearby nurses would come help me through it. If there were two in a fifteen minute period, I had to go straight to the emergency room. I argued with one of the nurses keeping a close watch on the timing of my contractions. "That one wasn't intense." I'd tell her, not really convincing anyone that I was not in labour.

December 2007. I had another dream: "We need you now."

I was working with a child with Down syndrome and he was on a manic search for something. It was close by and he wanted to give it to me. It was a national secret; the president was on the phone encouraging us not to look for it. Suddenly, helicopters swarmed the house, so I closed the curtains and turned off the lights and we left out the back door and went through the forest. The boy gave me a candy as we walked, a Swedish berry, my favourite. The taste was so sweet in my mouth.

We made it through the forest; it was time for him to go to school. I saw a ragged old woman on the sidewalk as we were hopping over dirty puddles and trash. She appreciated that we had brought her back to the basics of having fun even in chaos.

The boy said "I don't want to go to school. I need to keep looking."

"What are you looking for?" the old woman inquired.

"It is a special document." I told her.

"Is it this folder?" she asked.

I looked her in the eyes, so old and tired yet full of knowledge and wisdom. I opened the file. It had pages of all the angelic hierarchal information, from Metatron to the masonites. It was full of pictures, profiles, individual applications, roles and responsibilities. It was too much valuable information to be kept in one spot.

"Why are you giving it to me?" I asked.

"It is time." She nodded. "I need your help."

"Why me?" I stammered as I looked up from the file.

"Don't you know who you are?" she said, staring deep into my eyes. I felt her inside me, my body expanding full of breath and holding it. I felt my body fill with healing energy. "Say your name." she tells me.

"Angela Michelle." I responded, now lucid.

"Angel Michael," she tells me, "we need you back."

We were no longer on the street, but in my room. I was fully awake.

"Didn't you hear me? – We need you back." Her voice was just as strong without the facade of the dream in front of me.

"But I chose to come to Earth for a reason. I must fulfil that." I responded.

"Time is running out." she said.

"Then use me in my dream time." I offered.

"It's not enough. We need you back now." She was insistent.

"Earthly life is but a few short moments. I will be there soon and right now I need to be with my family."

From that point, the dreams seemed to greatly slow down. There continue to be coincidences that seem to put me in the right place at the right time to learn the lessons needed. I shifted my focus to my growing family and to being with them in the moment.

Days turned into weeks and suddenly there I was at 37 weeks, with full rights restored. The baby would be close to five pounds: that was full term! I started going to meetings and other events again, out of my office. I felt safe. *I woke up with regular contractions every five to seven minutes, sometimes breaking for about ten minutes then starting again…I still went to the seminar I had booked for this morning! I gave the instructor a heads up and just wrote down times on my paper. I sat with a nurse who was also a labour coach. She helped me through a series of intense contractions when I grabbed her arm and started crying. That one was too much. It lasted over two minutes and seemed unending. The pain was easily a level eight. Class stopped, and they called Eric. He was working down the street and got there in less than ten minutes, but all went quiet again. He drove us home.*

The weekend was quiet and I went back to work on Monday. It continued like this until the due date. December 23rd he came out. That little guy was right on his due date. I finished work the previous Friday and took some vacation time. Eric and I spent Friday night trying to induce labour; they say a G-Spot orgasm is the best way. Well, the contractions became regular. I think my pregnancy taught me to be patient, so we didn't tell anyone. We waited until five o'clock Saturday afternoon to give Christine a call. We waited until ten at night to call Emily, just in case we needed to go into the hospital. We told her this was likely it, but with this pregnancy who knew. Labour got intense.

I loved round two of delivery! He actually followed the plan, well, for the last few hours; let's not reflect on the past three months! We stayed home and I can honestly say I was blanked out, in a trance or asleep through most of it. I remember at one point wiping my face, wondering why it was so sweaty. I was focused on letting my body do what it needed to, to get this baby out. Christine and Eric remember it being a bit more intense than I do, but they didn't have the same adrenaline rush and endorphins kicking in. I don't remember telling Christine "If I'm not over 3cm, I'm going to kill you!"

I do remember telling her "If this isn't transition, we are going to the hospital."

"You've been transition for almost 20 minutes; it's almost over." She told me.

Evan Alister (following the same naming pattern, this time with shorter names because he is younger) joined our world at 4:08am December 23rd, 2007. The umbilical cord was wrapped around his neck and in a true knot, just like his brother's. That kid was active. His colour was fine, his breathing was fine and everything was good. His gooey little body was placed skin-to-skin on my chest and our love instantly bonded.

Emily came in and took a bunch of photos. We tried to wake up Ethan.

"But it's the middle of the night!" he said and reluctantly came in to the room to see his baby brother.

I got up, had a shower, and came back to a clean, warm bed to snuggle the sleep with my husband and baby. I fell asleep while Emily watched Ethan and took great pictures of the new big brother proudly holding our new baby.

Evan was a calmer baby, so my tears were nowhere near as bad this time. However, he such a ferocious eater, he ripped my nipples open and they bled! He grew so fast he was going to be huge!

The funny thing is that these boys match their labour and delivery. Ethan is often calm and cool then suddenly blows up, whereas Evan always puts us in panic mode and then things turn out ok. Evan was walking at nine months. By a year, he was climbing up onto the kitchen counters using the knobs on the drawers and jumping off of the sofa, but he would always land without injury. Ethan, on the other hand, managed to get a concussion and 15 stitches and has had Norwalk, Roseola, H1N1 and any other bug that has come around.

Very early on, they both started to demonstrate strengths. Ethan could use a computer and mouse at 18 months. He navigated kids' games and showed great visual attention and memory. He has always been able to figure out puzzles and games quickly. Evan, however, is completely physical; he was running and kicking a ball before he was 18 months. He could master whatever sport was presented to him – Frisbee, soccer, and baseball, all before he was two years old.

People assumed he was older simply based on his size. Strangers would offer their evaluation of his speech and language, telling us that he was delayed. I would always respond saying "Actually, he is doing quite well for his age." I would then tell them how old he was and ask; "How old is yours?" Their child who at most was Evan's height was often one or two years older than him. By age two, he was three and a half foot tall. The doctor told me he will likely be over seven feet tall. A friend did some basic research and told me that about one in four people who are over seven feet tall are in the NBA – interesting odds. I've been using that as an incentive for him to eat his protein and veggies.

May 15th, 2008. *It is so hard breaking the cycle. The first time I yelled at Ethan, I had to take a step back and laugh. I was yelling at my four year old, frustrated with my six month old. This was ridiculous.* A few months later he misbehaved and I took away all electronics.

"I hate you!" he yelled at me.

All I could do was look back at him and with the same level of intensity I responded with "Well if all you hate me for is taking away electronics, we are doing, ok aren't we?" But it got easier to yell and easier to brush off. I tried using the philosophies and practices from my training and feared that the neurological pathways and firing synapses were beyond my control.

When Ethan was six, he went through a retaliation period that drove me crazy. *I let him into my childhood. How much is too much for a six year old? I'm not sure, but I told him that my dad would have belted me, and I wouldn't have been able to sit down. I never could have treated my parents with that much disrespect or retaliated after a punishment. He was near tears. Perhaps that was too much information…he needed it. I think my childhood also made me over-critical of Eric's parenting. Eric is a* great dad, strict sometimes, but he would never do to our children anything close to what was done when we were children.

Jennifer's daughter came to visit my mom in August 2009 and my mom thought it was a good idea to stop by my place.

"Would you like a glass of wine with dinner?" I offered.

"My mom doesn't want me to drink until I'm of age." she said as she declined.

"Well if you are going to try, it is best to do in a safe location. Alcohol started showing up at my parties in grade seven." I was baffled that she hadn't been exposed to alcohol at 16 years of age.

I reflected on that visit with my niece, and wondered about the lack of relationship I have with her mom. Is there something worth saving? Is it worth reconnecting? It normally only takes a moment before the truths pop the thought bubble. How can I be present and grounded in an interaction in which so many questions, anger and resentment persist? The transparency I crave in relationships would be fogged.

My plan was to make our house the "fun house" we did a big renovation so kids want to hang out there. That way, as they get older and alcohol may start showing up at parties, I'll know and be able to continue educating. It's interesting what some people divulge, believe, and choose to do. I think that best part of parenting is having the chance to raise your kids with honesty and integrity, choosing to accept your past and teach your children in a way that gives them a better life.

Play dates make me aware of the diversity of families and remind me that mine had some normal components. *We had a boy over when Ethan was about five. At one point he asked Ethan, "What does your dad say when he's angry?"*

Ethan's response was so innocent. "He puts me in time out or yells sometimes."

The other boy responded "Oh, well my dad says words like; fuck, shit, crap, bitch and asshole." It was a list of words Ethan had never heard. I calmly told this boy we don't use words like that in our house.

There was another time when I offered Ethan, Evan and their friend some snacks, including some peanuts. The girl started laughing – "Get it, 'pee nuts'?" Ethan said "No, I don't get it." She continued, "Boys…nuts…" Ethan clearly didn't get it; he said "Yeah, and girls are nuts too!"

Very early on, Eric paid Ethan for creative thinking. It may have been a natural thing for him. One of my favourite memories of his creative reasoning followed a fight between Evan and Ethan. *Eric told Ethan, "If you are not happy with a situation, you need to remove yourself. You have control over your choices and by fighting with Evan you are also at fault. Go sit on the stairs in time out."*

Moments later, Ethan got up. "Sit down until your time out is finished." Eric instructed.

"But you said if I don't like it to walk away." Ethan said as he looked up.

This type of reasoning continued. Ethan was about eight years old and having a nonstop silly morning when Eric turned to him, a bit frustrated, and said "When are you going to stop acting like a child?"

Ethan looked at him, bewildered. "But Daddy, I am a child."

Evan is very physical and very sensory-based, and this also extends to music. He always wanted songs with loud bass, even when he was still inside me. *Evan was so funny this morning.* Imma Be *by the* Black Eyed Peas *came on the radio. He told me to turn it up. It was completely inappropriate. We often switched up some of the words and called it "Bumble bee." He asked for it to be louder and louder then sang "Bumble bee, bumble bee, bumble, bumble, bumble bee" while bopping his head around to the beat.*

He knows what the songs sound like and he doesn't like variations. I'm not allowed to sing his songs and others are not allowed to sing my regular song selections. One of my bedtime songs was played on the stereo, and Evan told the music system, "That's not right. You are singing it wrong."

Evan has continued to be judged based on his size. *Junior Kindergarten was almost over and I was told "His printing is not where it needs to be for a five-year-old."*

I smiled and said, "Good thing we still have another six months to work on it, then."

Evan was so physically coordinated that he fit in with the kids his size, rather than age, except for his social skills. He could do cartwheels and ridiculous jumps. He was five when he had his first intense sporting injury. It took about a week to heal, and then, only days after the scab fell off he said, "Look my face is all better. Now I can go destroy it again." As active and physical as he is, he has a keen interest in jewels. He keeps asking to buy gifts for his friends: bracelets, hair clips and gems.

Why the small rock? These boys love rocks, sand and beaches, so I picked it up one day at the beach. We were having a great day, and the rock, soft and smooth, made me smile when I touched it. I put it in my pocket then added it to my memory tin. It matched the one I took from the flower bed when we were looking at buying the house. The rocks remind me of simple things, and just existing in nature.

I think it was the boys that got me interested in family history. We were reflecting on stories from the past that die with the last storyteller. It was time to start getting those stories out of my Great Aunt Hilda. Suddenly my eyes viewed age completely differently. Those eyes, those wrinkles, and the grey hair – all of it was earned, and each contained a story. I started writing things down for the kids as a part of our family tree.

Her first story was about my mom's father. *He was with the NKVD, the Russian secret police. When the government asked him to hand over his dad for execution during a time of killing ministers, he refused and was classified as a traitor. He escaped Russia when the Germans invaded. After being classified as a traitor, he asked his wife and two children to come with him. She refused to join him, as she wasn't the traitor, he was. They went separate ways but never got a divorce. He met my grandmother shortly after the war, during the evacuation, having left The Caucasus. He wooed her, lied about his age and marital status, and they immigrated to Canada.*

Another great story was about Hilda's father, my mom's grandfather, who was born in the late 1890s. *He was a landowner and considerably wealthy. He took care of bees, she told me. He got more honey from bees in Siberia than he did in southern Russia. The flowers had more pollen. If he ever had a chance, he would put seeds in the ground in the morning, and they would be growing by evening, Hilda told me. When he refused to work for the state farm, the government burned his estate. They confiscated his land; the family had 24 hours to leave. With his remaining money, he moved and began another estate, which was also burned. With the little money he had remaining, he left Russia with his daughters Olga and Hilda.*

The previous generation, Hilda's grandparents (born in the 1870s) lived in Siberia. *She told me that some lived in tents others were dug into the sides of hills for added warmth for winter. In spring travellers would yell down the chimney, and help remove the snow, to dig the residents out of the homes. Hilda's stories sounded like they were bears trapped in a cave all winter long.* Sitting in front of my fireplace, I looked out at the snow-covered trees and the green path behind my house, and the 1870s seem almost unimaginable. How far the times have come and how much things have changed.

My mom told me some stories of my father's side. His paternal grandmother seemed most intriguing. *She was born in England. She had five children. She became a widow, and then remarried when she was 80 years old. She outlived her second husband, burying him when she was 82. When asked after the funeral, if she was planning to get married again and she responded, "No, it ties you down too much." The next 13 years she spent travelling to England and seeing North America by bus. She died at the age of 95, in 1981.*

His maternal grandmother was interesting too, but her story less was flattering. *She was born in Canada, and in 1935, after having 4 children; she abandoned the family and moved to the States, where she became the owner of a lucrative hotel. She remarried and when she died, nothing was passed on to the children.*

Eric's dad John was also completely into the idea of recording family history. John talked of his time on the farm. The story of his that spoke to me most was the one of John's grandparents on his father's side. *In the early 1900s they reached a point where they only had only one quarter left before starvation; on the farm, at that time 25 cents was equal to one week's worth of groceries. His grandmother said, "Put it in a safe spot." Then, as she gave it to her husband, it dropped and fell in a crack in floor boards of the log house. When the house was torn down it was discovered, given to John, and he passed it on to us. It is a Canadian 1883 quarter.*

There were a lot of stories about Eric's grandmother's death. John was one of eight siblings. It was so interesting to learn about all the observations surrounding the death, the division of siblings and speculation about what happened to the seemingly disappearing items of value.

Eric's mom was much quieter about the past. Her father was in the army. War changes people. She grew up as one of the youngest of nine children. They lived in Austria and she worked as a florist. She moved to Canada in 1966. Her mom died of cancer shortly after Heidi moved to Canada. So much life so filled of death. I was told Eric's grandfather never spoke of his time in World War II and I would never be brave enough to ask.

I often wonder what it is about me that will be remembered, what stories will make an impact and how they may influence others. The sequence of time, which for me moves so slowly, can hold so many stories, so many moments and they are all lost when the storyteller tells no more.

20

Holding On

anuary 2008. In my family, we've never had a terminal illness, except for my grandma, who was over 350 pounds and went quickly at the end. It was always quick, with no time to say goodbye. It was not that I embraced Eric's mom's illness, but rather the opportunity to slowly grieve. Shortly after Evan was born, she went into the hospital. She wanted to see him, so we made the trip. Her haemoglobin was low; they were keeping her for a few weeks. She celebrated her 60th birthday in the hospital. We tried to drive down every other weekend. Every time she got a blood transfusion, she looked better, felt better, but when she went home would deteriorate quickly. The family was hopeful. She tried surgery; they found a cancerous tumour that was too large to remove. She tried chemotherapy. There was still so much optimism.

After two subsequent fainting episodes and ambulance rides to the hospital, I started talking with the hospital staff to get updates before talking with Heidi. Things were not good. Her haemoglobin was as low as 40, only a week after getting nine units of blood. We tried to visit as much as we could with a newborn and three-and-a-half year old. We made the three and a half hour drive at least every three weeks. But she was getting tired. After she was transferred to the regional hospital, she decided she had had enough of hospitals. She wanted to go home. The pop tab was from a drink I had at the hospital, when I first realized that she wasn't getting better. I couldn't stop fidgeting with it.

It had been years since I'd had a tooth dream. Last night I dreamt I lost two teeth in one dream. The first was bloody and painful and the second I just found lying in my mouth, having fallen out without me noticing, but there it was when I spat out the blood from the first tooth. What was going to happen? Was it going to be Heidi and Hilda? Someone else was going to fade without me noticing?

The nurse confirmed my thoughts. They were providing palliative care. I found a private moment to talk with Heidi. "I know you are dying." I told her.

"I don't want the rest of the family to know. I want them to continue to have hope." she told me.

We talked about death and dying. "I want to die at home."

"That's ok; we just needed to make it legal." I told her.

I spoke with the home visiting nurse and requested a pronouncement so she would be allowed to die at home. We got a medical bed brought into the house and I encouraged her to get morphine on hand. The nurse agreed with me that morphine would be required in the near future. Heidi declined. We both told her she would need it at the end. She again declined, saying she didn't need it.

September 5ᵗʰ, 2008. What a day. I had just returned home after getting Ethan, who just finished his first week back to school, when we heard a thud. Part of the tree next door fell down on the power lines. When the fire-fighters showed up, they used a barrier tape to block off our house, the tree, and the power lines. We were not allowed to go into our home until it was deemed safe. It was a few hours before we were finally given the clearance to enter.

When finally allowed back in, I fed the kids, did laundry and prepared for our trip. Shortly after the kids went to bed, the phone rang. It was Heather, Eric's twin sister, she told us we needed to get on the road as soon as possible. With bags almost packed and kids asleep, we quickly loaded up the Jeep with sleepy boys and the weekend supplies. I drove as fast as I could. The script formed in my head in case I was pulled over by police. I would tell them the situation: "I'm so glad you pulled me over. I'd like this trip to be as safe as possible. I can't handle another life and death situation tonight. Could you please give me a police escort? I need to get my husband to his mom in time to say goodbye." I made it in less than 2.5 hours, but we were too late.

She fell into a pain coma, and died shortly after. It was a nasty, horrible night, but at least the dream now made sense. It was an emotional night of loss, tears, family and friends. I felt a bizarre comfort from being able to partake in the final states of a grieving process. I wonder about intent, plans, and timing. I really do feel that with birth and death, those who are meant to be there are the ones who are there. There are so many stories of people hanging on to say goodbye, and I wonder what the impact would have been had we made it in time. What would the boys have seen? What would they have remembered?

The next week, we lived out of the hotel as we did what we could to assist and prepare for the funeral. It was a challenge to deal with our emotions as we tried to explain death to Ethan, who was only four years old. Having only packed for the weekend, there were many supplies we needed. We tried to keep the boys busy and entertained.

He would ask, "Why is this all about her?" I'm not sure he got the finality of it. It made me wonder though, how would I want to go? Would I want it to be quick? With no chance for goodbyes or would I rather it be slow and painful...Would there be a way to keep my wits, not feel pain and still say goodbye?

21

I'm Normal

s I hold the pill container in my hand, I remember how much Ativan helped me through the worst of it. These tokens were critical in reinforcing memories of interactions that shaped whom I've become. My goal for so many years was to become normal, to be boring. These stories, the moments that seemed insurmountable and played such a critical role in my development and relationships, are simply becoming just that: stories. This mermaid was a drink topper from one of my favourite restaurants where I shared many of my stories and listened to those from others.

A part of me still wants to escape, hide out in survivalist mode, live off the grid, on a self-sufficient 20 acres of farmland. I keep looking for the perfect place and dream of doing it one day. But another part of me wants all the stories out, a testament to what a human can endure and where meaning is found. Perhaps it is also an attempt to give back and provide the support I've benefited from. Having someone to talk to, is truly the most important survival tool in life.

Every so often, little things still creep up on me. *Ethan got tall enough to ride a four loop roller coaster, he wanted me to go with him. I haven't been on an upside-down ride since grade four when my dad made me go on the "Rock and Roll" at the fairgrounds. I didn't want to go, but despite my crying, my dad made me. I threw up everywhere. They had to close the ride. It was horrible. I told Ethan the story from my childhood and why I was scared to ride. My adult mind knew I should try it. I told Ethan that I would ride it with him, but only for therapeutic value. Maybe choosing to ride a crazy upside down ride with someone I loved holding my hand would make it bearable. We went on, my fear started out at an eight out of ten as the ride began, but ended at a pitiful score of two. The ride that seemed to encompass so much, mentally, was nothing but a few loops. Another childhood fear was conquered. I asked him if he wanted to go again. He told me that coming straight down really fast was a little bit too scary for him. So we continued on to other rides.*

I went to a workshop on trauma and resiliency. One of the participants spoke of the moment she realized that material possessions mean nothing. "What does the sofa really matter, whether it's purple or not…" I responded that her comment was interesting because the material things are what I hold on to. My fire safe is filled with all of my photos and irreplaceable items. She went on about how it only really matters if your loved ones are ok. I went silent and pondered… maybe that's because my traumas normally involve losing the loved one and my relationship to material possessions is not in reference to a sofa, but to memories (like those pictured in this book) *as the few tokens I have of moments that remain as the only memories left.*

April 10th, 2010. Eric and I just celebrated our 10th wedding anniversary. It was planned ten years ago when a few friends said we should meet up ten years from now. Eric and I decided to renew our vows and exchange new rings with most of our original guests, back at the country inn where we got married. It was a great celebration! This time just it was one night, dinner and breakfast, but all costs were still covered in the invitation. We had a balloonist who created and gave instructions on how to create balloon animals, flowers and other items. An illusionist gave an after-dinner performance that left many wondering "How did he do that?" We hung out with drinks, and the guys with their cigars, reminiscing for hours. It was great to see everyone again and see how much our lives have changed over the past decade.

I think I'm finally at a point in my life at which things seem pretty perfect, even with the woes of child rearing. It's a stage I have always dreamt of. This moment seemed like an unobtainable utopia. I love and am married to a man who loves me. We have two healthy kids, a house with a big back yard and time to spend with each other.

August 22nd, 2010. We are losing Katya. She has been our path to solace for the last three years. It almost feels like I'm not only losing my child care provider, but also losing a friend, a daughter and a great support system. Yet it seems like we will never say goodbye. She insists we visit her every two weeks when she's at school. Katya is the reason this trip down memory lane started. I began reviewing my old journals to create a university survival guide for her, based on my experiences from my first years away from home. It then turned into a university survival kit, a box filled with all the things Eric and I thought she might need first year.

It was that review of old journals that got me back in touch with a few of the critical people from my past. I gave each of them an outline of some of the journal entries that made it into the guide and a review of some of the moments we shared that left memories I will always cherish. I took it as an opportunity to reconnect and offer thanks for helping to shape my life path. The responses varied as much as the stories did. There are a few friends who I am still in contact with. I just saw Amanda and Liz at our anniversary and got in touch with Becky with the anniversary invite. Amanda said some of the stories were too much. The silence from Liz was deafening. We shared so many good moments first and second year, including dancing at clubs and the trip to Alcatraz, but I guess thanking her for that night I was raped was too much…I needed her to reject me for my own growth. Perhaps my therapeutic purpose and growth was not appropriate, thanks. Alistair, the high school friend I trusted and loved more deeply than I had the mind to realize, was one I expected a response from. He remained silent for over a year. In my final attempt to contact him, I suggested it was indifference on his part and sent my thanks for the life lessons and great memories. It was that email to which he finally responded. We met for coffee and he seems like he is in a good space and still the amazing person he was years ago.

I also got in contact with many other friends who played lesser but still important roles in my journey; some from elementary school, like Tanya and Tracy, and Neil, some from high school, like Kevan and Sue; and a few others from university. Superficially, everyone seems to be doing well. With Joe, it was amazing how the reconnect happened. Slowly, I gave him more and more stories I had written as I came across him in my journal entries. The words "I will always love you" were finally reciprocated.

I had many texts and emails that became the main records of my daily life, rather than journals, as technology advanced. There are so many stories leading up to this big smear the previous month has become. Was it inevitable? Was it karma? On Valentine's Day, 2011, the high of our 10th anniversary was fading. Feeling unloved and underappreciated, I told Eric we needed to talk and tried to initiate the conversation.

February 15, 2011. *Ok, so I didn't think it was possible, but my lowest expectations were smashed. It was 8:45pm when he got home. The kids had been upstairs since 7:30pm, and were almost asleep after 45 minutes of reading. I had plenty of time to think while reading. What bothered me most was that list of five things that make us feel loved wanted and desired, and the discussed goal to try and do at least two of them. He read my list Sunday night. He knew little things made a difference. When he came home, he started complaining about work. He could have left his conversation about work at work. He didn't need to talk about it anymore.*

"It already has you all day and that's all you can talk about now? I want to hear about you missing us, or wanting to be with us, or something about how much you love me." I said.

"I'll try to make it up." he told me.

"It's done, let's just move forward." I feel like I've been confirmed as not being a priority in his life. I'm feeling less of a priority and more of a necessity. I need to get the kids, clean, cook and give physical satisfaction. But the emotion seems to be lacking.

He did send a text today. It sounded so forced. "Morning, Hope your day is going OK. I love you." It would have been enough yesterday, but today the words seem empty. What is love? Is a word sufficient without the emotion behind it? Maybe I'm too needy.

Anxiety is creeping back into my mind, taking over my thoughts. Today is March 7, 2011. What do I say? How do I say it? I feel like everything has been sucked out of me. I feel paranoid, like everyone is watching me, waiting for me to fail. I feel like there is nowhere to begin, nowhere to start, nowhere to end. Then what is this voyage? Am I supposed to be experiencing life to the fullest? And what happens when it all starts to spiral down?

Tuesday March 22nd, 2011. Joe is in town. We had met up Saturday for dinner, but he was still in town so we met up for lunch before he had to go. Today's visit had so many key topics. It's been crazy, intense and diverse. He was talking about instinctively saying he was 29, without thinking or intending to lie. He had recently turned 35, and I'm one month away. On reflection, it made me think about how many of those I have: truths, lies, embellishments, denials, realities. Who can tell the difference if I believe it to be true? Why does the mind sometimes focus on an alternate reality? Then, suddenly, these images come to mind, spinning me out of control. My brain feels exhausted. It was simple stuff, blown out of proportion.

What is it about being in close proximity to Joe opens me up to such vulnerabilities? It's a strong comfort and familiarity he brings that perhaps I innately know. He can handle my trauma and with that strength, I can handle anything. He was the one I first started telling my stories to, so I guess there are simply more stories to be remembered. Perhaps I'm stable enough now to be shaken up again.

I had a memory of waking up, with disturbing actions, pretending to sleep, believing I'm asleep, convincing myself in the morning it was a dream. Was it? Which times? If I wrote them down now, would that validate their occurrence? Do I need to validate their existence? It was so many years ago, and yet keeping the experiences secret seems to keep them strong, unspoken truths I try to convince myself never happened. When will these flashbacks of long-hidden childhood memories end? Some I can accept, others scare me, and all remind me how messed up my childhood was. I was seven or eight, Jennifer was living with us, Billy had his room in the basement and he had a friend over. I don't remember Emily being present. It seemed a natural, normal, familiar game: run around and catch me. Tag, right, that was innocent enough, but then I remembered how it ended. Catch…kiss…strip…crap! Why are there so many flashbacks? When will they stop?

We had such messed up childhood games. I can see that now. I actually liked the game of stretch. It was the poor man's version of Twister. You play outside with a steak knife and have to throw it so that it sticks into the ground. You have to be able to stretch to put a body part where it stuck in, keep your balance, remove the knife and throw it back into the ground for the other participant to have a turn. If the knife doesn't stick in the ground the person that would have had to put a body part there gets one body part free. If you get stabbed, you get all parts free.

Suddenly, I feel like I'm losing touch with reality. Reality is a social construct, too. Does this moment exist? If I think, does that mean I exist? I'm so paranoid of where I am, who's watching me – who are the potential threats? Who am I? Am I who I was or am I who I project? At what point does choice play a role? At what point am I considered a cognitive being aware of my surroundings and my environment and able to make conscious decisions? Where is that border between the images I am seeing and my life? Where are the boundaries of reality and how do they intercept with beliefs? I'm feeling a bit schizophrenic right now. Yet, I have to ask, is identifying the feeling making me any more conscious of it? Does that validate or exclude the potential to be schizophrenic? Any situation defined as real is real in its consequences...are my secrets then defined as real? If I dismiss them, does that mean they never happened? My brain is not accepting of the secrets not yet dealt with.

I attempt to rationalize. After a while, I adapted to my environment, and normalized it. My abnormal actions were normal in the abnormal world I had become accustomed to. But it's not normal. It's messed up. Who plays sex games like that?

What was even scarier was that the flashbacks didn't stop. As Joe drove me home, my mind was exploding. Suddenly there was another abuser in the basement, pinching our nipples. The story was dwarfed by the next image. I think I needed a victim memory to help with the flash that was next. I was the abuser. Fighting, touching. I did it. I am a monster.

I can't deal with this! I need a distraction. I couldn't say goodbye to Joe. I couldn't be alone. Should I tell him? I tried to talk, distracted myself and invited him in, gave him a tour. The images are holding on to me now, even after he's left. I had gone to sleep in her bed. That was normal sleepover stuff, but I woke up touching her. She was asleep, so they were touches she never consented to. I froze as I became conscious. What was I doing? How did I do that in my sleep? Did she wake up? Did she pretend to sleep? Does she remember? How has my past worked its way into my subconscious? Why was I being haunted with it years later?

At what point do I become responsible for my actions? At what point do these flashbacks stop? How much more is there to remember? What other actions have I blocked out from my memory? As the memories fight to be seen, I fight to bury them. I'm terrified by the shift from victim to abuser. I'm thankful for the years of therapy and thankful to be in a safe space. But it sucks to be alone. I called Eric. He's pissed that Joe drove me home. My flashbacks went untold, so I felt deserving of the memories and solitude. I am a freak.

"I'm normal!" the words screaming to be heard inside my head. But I only feel as normal as a crazy person with two fingers up their nose. I remind myself of the training I had regarding abuse…some children make up a fantasy life to escape the world they live in. How different is that from schizophrenia? Is this my escape from reality, due to childhood abuse? Is it a coping mechanism? How different is that from normal people getting absorbed in a movie, book, concert or dramatic performance for a few hours to escape reality or to enjoy another's creativity? What if I design my own fantasy and creativity and purposefully get sucked into distractions? Is that so unhealthy?

I'm in the midst of another crazy panic attack I'm trying to talk myself out of. It's April 7th and I still haven't told anyone about my flashbacks. I feel so stressed, anxious, worried, with panic and paranoia covering me… It started yesterday on the train ride home, with crazy paranoid thoughts of my dad's murder. Last night, watching TV before bed seemed fine but the content was too close to home. My dreams were fine, but then I heard a voice this morning saying "hey" in a quiet, creepy whisper. It feels like the quiet creepy feeling has followed me.

I couldn't find my subway tokens this morning. They ended up being under the microwave, but it set me back a few moments. I ended up running to catch the bus to get the first train, and as I was running, the fear saturated me. Running to or running from? Fear covered me. The bus was pulling away but then stopped for me. I kept running, even on the bus, but my mind and body fought to run and I fell. My heart was pumping from the running, fear and panic-based thoughts. I feel like I need to keep running, but to where and from what? I'm on the verge of tears. Is it my dad, the 19th year of imprisonment, our anniversary, my birthday, getting older, my ghosts, the flashbacks, it's all just pouring in to one big nasty paranoid, flashback meltdown.

Trying to find peace through God, I tried journaling on the ride to work. It's not helping. I tried jumping into work; it's not helping. I've cried; it's not helping either. This sucks. Maybe sending the thoughts will help. I sent the journal entry to Eric, but I feel so alone and afraid right now. He responded quickly and tried to talk me down, but I'm so far gone, nothing is helping.

It is April 27th. What a crazy day! I was listening to music on the subway (blocking out the Rastafarian guy singing loudly about trying to change the world) when a young woman jumped up on the seat, pressing the emergency button three or four times. I quickly walked down to see if I could help. A woman I recognized as a regular on the first train was sitting in a reclined limp position. I patted her leg. "Are you ok?" I pat much harder, her arm, her face. Nothing. I check her neck for a pulse...nothing. I keep trying to rouse her, thinking "Oh crap, what if she's dead?" The crowd was gathering around me. It was likely only about 45 seconds but it felt like forever. Her eyes slowly opened – she looked like she was a drunken, angry, pissed-off crazy person, not whom I saw when she got on the train. "Are you ok?" I asked.

She looked around, bewildered. "You are on the subway heading southbound. Are you ok?" I continued.

"I feel like I'm going to faint." she muttered, her eyes softening.

"I think you did." I told her, so thankful she was alive. I took her head and leaned it on my shoulder. She was hot, sweating and very slow to speak. I kept talking, trying to gather some info. She looked about 50.

Apparently it had happened before, but it had been about a year since the last episode. She has high blood pressure and is on medication; she didn't have breakfast. (Interpretation: it was likely very low blood pressure that caused the fainting and my inability to detect the faint pulse.)

We arrived at the next station. The subway train engineer called for a doctor or nurse to assist while we await EMS. A nurse, whom I'd call a bit to full of herself, jumped in and suggested we try to move the victim to a reclined position. The woman had not yet regained enough stability to sit up unsupported, and declined the position change. The nurse started asking a bunch of questions. She seemed so much more intense than I was and didn't want to listen to the history I'd already gotten. A doctor showed up, who did want to hear the history. He listened and agreed with my interpretation. A few minutes passed and she felt good enough to get off the train so it could move forward. I sat with her on a bench. She asked for help taking her coat off and as the trains passed by she said the cool breeze helped too. Everyone showed up: fire-fighters, EMS, transit officers and police. After the EMS finished taking her vitals, I gave her my strawberries to help get her blood pressure a bit higher, and we sat for a while, her numbers slowly improving.

After an intense morning, my reflection is focused on how many others gathered. I was about half a train car's length away and was the first to check her out and try to wake her? I wondered about timing, whether I was in the right or wrong spot at the right or wrong time. After beginning my day at work I was with a patient, in the middle of something, when a doctor and ECG technician came in to do rounds and told me (with a bit too much attitude) to leave, indicating it was a bad time. The nurse tried to ease their intent to display power and control. She told them "Angela was already in the room and just needs a moment to finish."

Apparently, they didn't feel the need to respond to her wasted words. Since they only needed the mom, the nurse decided to take the baby out of the room for me so I could finish. Perhaps my thoughts are about how people handle situations, and how that changes depending on the situation, the urgency of action and emotional attachments to the outcome.

One of the kids at Ethan's school had their mom die recently, so he's been asking a lot of questions. At dinner he asked about what would happen if his mom or dad died. Eric responded, "You would have a new daddy within two years."

I looked at him. "Two years?" I said, dumbfounded.

"Well, it's one month of grieving for every year of the relationship, so that's just over a year in total. I'm sure you'd move on." he said.

"Wow..." I responded, attempting to gather my thoughts.

He continued, saying "If mommy died I'd likely live out the rest of my years alone."

"Ok." I interjected, "that's not healthy. First of all, I would hope you'd have some kind of a support network to help you through whatever trauma may have happened, resulting in my demise. Second, I'd hope you would eventually deal with the pain and learn to love again. I can't imagine getting the kids a new daddy within two years, but I can definitely see myself having a support network to help me through whatever happened." I went on to talk about how important he is to the kids and that his impact on their development is critical to influence who they are becoming.

I then reaffirmed for Ethan that if anything ever happened, and it likely wouldn't for a very long time, someone would be here to take care of him. He then asked "What if you both died?"

"Emily and Mark would care for you." I told him.

"What if they died?" he continued.

"Then Urs and Mike would watch you." I responded.

"And if they died?" he asked.

"Likely Grandma." I said.

"But she'd be like 120 years old!" he responded.

"Oh, then you'd be about 60 years old, so maybe you'd have a wife and kids at that point." I tried to catch up to his thought process.

"No, I'll kick my kids out when they are 20. Maybe I'd just move into one of those homes for really old people like Aunt Hilda." he said, seemingly content.

Wow. I love the way his brain works. Hilda is 78, and moved into a retirement home. I'm sitting here now wondering why with some situations the right path is so obvious and easy to choose and with others, not so much. Home life has been so complicated lately. I have a good friend who today reminded me that so many others would be envious of my current state of life. I'm not worried about money, health or being abused. If my biggest issue is not feeling wanted and desired I have a pretty good life.

Still, I ran away from my problems and started focusing on my friends' problems. I started meeting up with friends for lunch, for drinks, after work or evenings, as often as it was possible. I found I needed a social network and people to talk to. I'm baffled to learn how many people are unhappy with their sex lives. Seems like it's one of the few aspects of my life I am happy with!

Not sure if I'm turning into a sex therapist…but it seems like there are so many basic aspects to a good sex life that people are overlooking. The chats seem to have helped a few friends in building awareness, and improving quality. It really all comes down to finding out what you like, getting your partner to do it, and reciprocating.

Most commonly it was the woman not being satisfied. I have two friends that achieve better orgasms with a toy than they do with their partner, and many others who say things like they just want him to finish so it would be over. Having been through moments of not liking my body, including rape, pregnancy, and flashbacks, I know how important it was for me to learn to like my body vicariously through Eric liking my body. It was those unexpected warm gentle touches that reinforced how much he liked me. It seems strange to realize how many people seem to forget about the sensuous nature of skin and how much a touch can hold.

My chat today covered almost everything. It's funny when women are more aggressive than the guys, and having to reverse the roles and tell her to start slow. I suggested she monitor the interest of her partner and explore together. A good massage may lead to a happy ending after one massage or it may take several smaller baby steps to get there. I think everyone should be able to feel pleasure and enjoy the connection a touch contains. But it's not always that easy. Body memory often sets me back with thoughts that prevent me from a total mind release and the ability to be present in the moment to maximize the pleasure.

I was chatting with another friend who was having some challenges. When offering ideas, I suggested some simultaneous clitoral stimulation to increase her enjoyment, and she disclosed that she had been a victim of female circumcision, more accurately known as female genital mutilation. I can't imagine loving a part of my body and learning to feel the pleasure in something that was culturally shamed and removed. Horrifying thoughts, images and memories prevent so many women from enjoying simple things like a pleasure organ. I wonder how many women have thought patterns that inhibit total enjoyment.

In my writing, I've come to realize a few basic truths. One is that suffering provides an opportunity for growth and change. A good friend likes to remind me "If you are having a good time, enjoy it, because it will pass. If you are having a rough patch, enjoy it, because it too will pass." Eric said the same thing back in university: "Things we had challenge us (as a child) pale in comparison to those that we seem to face now [just as in some future time, the trials of now will pale to those of the future]." I love that I have so many reminders to live in the present moment and accept it for what it is: another life moment.

It's strange to look back on years of trauma and see a process of how such important life lessons arose from such horrid experiences. Yet somehow, it's impossible to look back without realizing it all had a purpose. Had I not had the childhood abuse, I wouldn't have questioned religion and spirituality, which led to many supernatural experiences in childhood. Had Jennifer not been so mean to me, I never would have made it to the different high school, determined to make more of my life. Had my father not been murdered, I wouldn't have had the push or financial ability to leave town. Had I not been raped, it would have taken much longer to be ready to choose a safe boyfriend, which led to my marriage and kids. Every moment you are alive is an opportunity to reflect on your path and choose to change it or to reinforce the goals you are working towards.

I thought about the high school entry about "what I'd trade for just a moment of pure happiness, where nothing could remind me of the pain and trouble I've experienced" and the entry from the day with my spiritual advisor. "I guess in simplest terms, I want love, happiness and to not have to worry about money. I want to work towards boring. I want to have enough money to buy what I need and most of my wants. I want to love and be loved equally." Well, I think I've mostly achieved that. Having written those and reflecting on where I've been and where I am simply reinforces another basic truth: happiness is on a spectrum, and my standards for happiness have changed. The threshold of happiness changes as proximity to obtaining happiness is approached. Once a series of moments has been experienced, the expectation for more increases. I am in a state in which I believe I am experiencing a more acceptable range of normal moments of happiness and frustrations. In early June 2011, *a guy on the train approached me and said "You look like a well adjusted individual."*

I laughed. "Yes, years of therapy can do that to you."

"Can I ask you a question?" he asked.

"Sure." I responded.

He had a scenario from the news he wanted to discuss (kids driving off, dragging a police officer) to get an opinion, and thought I was a good person to ask, a well-adjusted individual. Ha! I made it. I'm normal.

22

That's Life

I have no idea how or why some tokens call to me. This morning was one of those mornings. It feels like there is a message I need to get. Sitting on a bench I noticed a tile beside me. It was part of a bigger picture, unnoticed for its individuality but fallen and now standing alone. It seemed to call to me, spoke about beauty and importance, as well as the fragility and fluidity of glass in its changing states of matter. I had way too much time this morning after what was such a crazy month. Forced to slow down, I got to spend time on my email catching up, enjoying some peace at Second Cup. I then returned to discover my first parking ticket. I showed up early for a full day communication workshop, confirming another relationship is ready to heal. Then, while driving home, I got a chip in my Jeep's windshield.

That glass tile reminded me that life is always changing. My life is always changing. So much has been said, so many stories told, and yet after multiple reviews of the journals, it seems like it's just not enough. I've always said I craved normalcy or a boring life. Yet I feel that it will never be in my cards.

If I'm not happy I need to change. So what does life change mean? What would my therapist say? June 12, 2011, I tried a mock therapy session.

"What holds you together?" he would ask.

"I will not leave my kids, or take them from their dad. He's not putting them in harm's way. He takes them to the park, and he reads bedtime stories." I'd say.

"So what is the issue?" he would ask.

What would I tell my therapist? That it's the little things? Daily challenges of not feeling loved. Really only seeing him for a few hours each evening, with little to no contact during the day, and when I do see him it's full of him venting about crap at work, crap with kids. I'm sick of it. Sure I get an "I love you" here and there, but words are empty without behaviour to back it up. Sex is good, likely the only time I feel connected and likely why I'm holding back. Does he even notice? Do I use sex to fill a void? But Eric was there for me during all my crap. How long can I stay in his? How long do I have to? Eric is getting challenging; we've had progressively more and more arguments.

It's Tuesday, June 14th, 2011. I feel like I need to talk, and yet I also just want it to blow over. Sunday, I got into a big fight with Eric. He lost his temper with the kids, and I said I wouldn't tolerate that. I had enough of my own childhood abuse. Eric is a million times better than my dad is, but I am sensitive to any abuse. The look in his eyes as he yelled scared me.

It's time to start calling in resources. I reminded him of child development at three years of age: Evan is only developmentally capable of listening about 50% of the time.

Wednesday, he acted like nothing's happened. I feel myself growing further and further from him. We are no longer a team, no longer a unified front. Ever feel like you just want to escape from your life for a while? *Maybe I'll start bath and story time earlier to reduce exposure and give him an extended cool down period. Maybe we all just need a break.*

A big bright neon sign is screaming at me. I'm sure one day it will seem funny how life keeps changing the goals as experiences change the preferred route. Today, June 17th, started so normal, I was having a regular physical with my doctor until my pap. She continued with the regular chatty questions and life updates as she prepared to do the swabs, but then her line of questioning changed to be a bit more direct.

"Hmm, you have a bit of yeast." she commented. She then corrected herself. "No, that's not yeast, there's something else going on." She then asked, "How many sexual partners do you have?"

Baffled, and hardly keeping up with her, I said "In the last 14 years? One."

"Well it might just be bacterial vaginosis, or it could be trichimonis. I'm just going to do a few extra swabs." Time blurred as she spoke. "Do you have any reason to think Eric might be cheating on you?"

My head was spinning; that was such a loaded question. Do I have any reason? Does she know my brain works in scatter plot, criminal investigation mode? So he was late coming home on Valentine's Day, there was the double date with his friend from work and her boyfriend, we saw Serendipity. Suddenly, any and every conceivable opportunity for him to have had the opportunity filled my mind. Now I was questioning everything: time, truth, fidelity, and friends.

I was supposed to be having lunch with John afterwards. John was friend who happened to be a doctor. I was thankful that I had plans with someone who had a medical background and able to deal with people in crisis modes. I wasn't planning to go into details, but as our talk continued,

I noticed I was talking about nothing and it was driving me crazy. Of all the people I know, he was someone who could deal with the medical and the emotional components of what I was going through. I told him. We talked about anything and everything else it could have been, and he tried to reinforce my trust in Eric but also validated my concerns, encouraged me to wait and see what happened next and tried to calm me down. But its eight o'clock, the kids went to bed for the night and I can't wait any more. How do I start that conversation? "Hey, the doctor thinks I have a sexually transmitted infection (STI). I know where my body's been; where has yours been?"

I'm going to mess it up. I don't know how I can do this and not sound like I'm telling him it's him and not me. How can I allow for that trust to be shaken? If I don't tell him I will still be sitting here alone in my fears, freaking out. I need some comfort. Would I believe him if he said he hasn't been with anyone? What if he says that and it comes back positive? Then I have to deal with and STI and him lying to my face? Balance...limits... changes...It's so messed up. I have to go talk to him.

It went as well as it could have. He said he hasn't been with anyone, and I told him right now I believe him. My concern is that if the test comes back positive, I'm not sure what I'll believe.

"As stupid as it sounds. I would have preferred the answer to be yes, because at least then you could have told me it was in the past, it was over and we'd have somewhere to move forward from. If it came back positive it would make sense. Now, if it comes back positive there will be a trust concern...and I won't know what to think." I continued.

He was disappointed by that, but he agreed that it made sense. There were some apologies and I thanked him for the talk, which ended with "I hope everything will be ok." We fell asleep holding hands. It was so much better than I anticipated.

Clearly, I get too emotionally involved. Last week, on June 14th I went in to talk to this mom and check out her baby. She was bonding and everything seemed to be going well. I had suspicions of a syndrome and needed to follow up, so planned to revisit her the following day. The following day I went back, but the baby was already taken to intensive care and the mom was in tears. We talked for about an hour. Thursday the syndrome was confirmed. I finished the tests, and the mom was crying in my arms. She considered the syndrome a bad omen, karma, and a symbol of guilt; she thought it was all her fault. Wishing she aborted and unable to cope, she was considering putting the baby up for adoption.

Today, June 21st, I noticed the baby was still there. I went to check in and see how things were going. The mom was gone and the baby was in the care of Children's Aid. I put the information about the follow up in her file, and then noticed her mom had named her Angela. We had spent a lot of time talking Thursday and Friday, but it was one of those things. She had asked me if I would choose to have a child with Down syndrome. We talked about how everyone wants a healthy baby, but yes, if I had to choose, I do prefer children with Down syndrome to any other special need. I talked about how there is such a big spectrum of capability and potential, and about how loving children with Down's can be, giving so many big hugs compared to children with autism, for example, whose eye contact is rare and gentle touches infrequent.

It felt like the mom had left a message in her name; a message of choice and help. Was it because I'd choose her? Is that why she's called Angela? Because I listened to mom, hugged her, gave her tissues? I wanted to take the baby home, love her and help her reach her best potential, then give her back to her mom and say see she is beautiful, she is amazing and she can do anything she wants! Yet I walked away today with a sad heart only to hope the parents that adopt her give her every opportunity to succeed.

It is still Tuesday June 21st. My doctor called me to say the results were in, they were negative, but she wanted me back in on Friday. She said she didn't know what it was, and the other swabs could have dried up. She checked me out and told me "It's still there, so I'm going to take more swabs and repeat all the tests."

She then asked, "Do you want me to treat it?"

"Hell yeah!" I said!

"I'm going to be aggressive and give you two prescriptions that treat everything from Bacterial Vaginosis and Trichimonis to Chlamydia."

I was a mess. I called Eric and he said he couldn't come home early, had something he needed to finish at work. I assumed he needed to tell his girlfriend. What work is more important than this? I went and got my prescriptions. Katya was with the kids. I thought maybe beta blockers would help. Feeling like crap, questioning my life, my relationship, my supports, my trust, and my future, I drank; it was the next best thing. Don Julio was my best friend for the next half hour. Oversized shot glasses assisted, and six shots later I was in tears, and Katya was holding me. John and a friend from work were the only other people who knew anything was going on and both were on the phone, doing what they could to stop the spiral.

Finally Eric was on his way home and tequila was erasing the emotional impact of another trauma in my life. The room started spinning. I threw up, snuggled and cried in Katya's arms and spent the evening questioning reason, purpose and existence. Anger turned to acceptance and I turned quiet. Eric got home, insisted there was no one else, but I was in no mood to talk to him. In an attempt to reground myself and find my spiritual path, I began bargaining with God. I did a ton of Reiki and promised to rid myself of hate. I turned to walks in the park, feeling the energy from the trees and nature.

The next check-up my doctor told me that whatever it was, it was unresponsive to treatment and she was sending me to a specialist. Being on a priority list for a specialist bothered me, but after a quick check and an ultrasound, the specialist said "I'm not so concerned about the spots on your cervix."

Then he continued, "A bigger concern is this growth on your ovary." Oh my God, there's more? It's worse? He sent me for tests and told me what to look for, when to go to the emergency room. He had concerns about my ovary getting too heavy and twisting. This sucks. The growth is 4.5cm, and they operate at 5.0cm. He was going to closely monitor it at various times in my cycle over the next month.

After all of that questioning of faith and trust and my relationships, suddenly I was sent into a whole other whirlwind. He dismissed whatever was on my cervix. Does that mean it is not an STI? I had to start trying to discuss the shaken trust and repair my relationship with Eric, while feeling lost and alone in my battle. Would an STI have been better? Was the cancer I wished for so many years ago coming to fruition? I focused on the lighter aspects, such as my second ultrasound and the lovely woman performing transvaginal procedure, pressing on my lower belly from inside and out and telling me I had really nice skin. Could I flirt back? Comment on her wand technique? I decided to let it go.

I have had an amazing opportunity with a new job for the last six months, and I feel like I have something to offer the profession. I am working with the expert in the field, one of the few people I've ever put on a pedestal. I had a meeting with Martyn, and I evidently said something he deemed helpful. He said "And that's why I love you." Martyn says the words with ease, words that I searched for through every document from my dad and couldn't find. Is it wrong to want him to fill that void? His words heal my heart a little more every time I hear it. I wonder what it would have been like to have a dad that was as supportive and encouraging as Martyn is to me. Love: the meaning is contained within the word, the way we define it and the intensity of the emotions provoked by it. How do we define a dad? A dad is a positive male role model, a source of love and affection, someone to encourage your growth and development, and someone who is there for you when you are down. Martyn is all of that. Around him, I feel valued and purposeful, like I am worthy to join him on that pedestal I see him on. His hug today meant so much to me.

The circle of people who know what's going on right now is so small. I'm starting to feel like I need to let people in. I called Emily. We went out for dinner last night. I broke down as soon as she asked how I was. I told her the story. Today was my follow-up after the ultrasound done by the other clinic. Hemorrhagic what? I was ok with the word cyst, but "likely a benign growth?" It's too much.

I continued on my spiritual journey and bargaining with God. I had to work towards ridding myself of hate and forgiving those for whom I held a grudge. As I did, I seemed to achieve further milestones. I think one of the hardest people to forgive was my sister Jennifer. I realize that we all seek out self preservation through different paths. She experienced so much more trauma than I ever did. I guess I always had issues with the mindset that certain people were supposed to protect you. Again and again I was let down. I needed to accept my belief that she was supposed to protect me was couldn't be fulfilled, and that my path was my journey and I was the one who needed to be there for me. I started working on forgiving my father when I was sixteen, and it took almost fifteen years! With Jennifer, every time I attempted to forgive her I was re-traumatized, so I just kept putting it off.

Driving home, Madonna came on my playlist and I suddenly I found my thoughts absorbed in a happy memory of Jennifer, Emily and I; singing and swinging in the park. I realized that my perception, thoughts and feelings about the relationship only really affected me, and if I control my consequences why choose to carry around hatred? I started focusing on this thought and considered drafting an email to share the memory.

Falling asleep I thought about how to phrase that email. I felt someone taking what felt like sheets of fog off of me, feeling lighter and lighter.

"Hey what are you doing?" I asked.

"It's time." the voice said. Lighter and lighter still, I started floating up off of my bed, through the roof, lighter and lighter as more fog was being lifted from me. I'm a light in the shape of an oval, flying up through the sky. I feel someone holding my hand. We arrive at a doorway. "She's ready." the voice tells what I can only guess is a gatekeeper.

"Yes, great progress, but not quite yet. There is still something else she needs to do." the gatekeeper said. Peace came over me. I was suddenly back in my bed, warmth and love covered me in a cocoon and I fell asleep.

I was in a dreamless state. I woke up feeling refreshed and more aware. Everything looked crisp, like I had on new glasses. Yet still there were those words reminding me there was something else I need to do. Who knows what

I have left to do. There is now more love in my life that I have ever known. My support network is growing and I would say that, other than Eric, there are five very close friends I love dearly. Each is unrelated and in a different circle of friends. Sure, borders sometimes blur and perhaps that is what I need to work on, but to define a friendship and levels of relationships to one who has had such a messed up experience is challenging. There are different kinds of love, such as a love for a parent, for a child, for a spouse, all with very different aspects of intimacy, affection and acceptable behaviours. Having never known unconditional love, trusting, feeling, and loving continue to surprise me.

The growth is gone! Sometimes that happens, the doctor told me. Amazing! I sent a group text. The response from John forced introspective celebration. "Great! Thanks for letting me know. So very happy for you (all). Will have a beer on you (yes, I have some). Now remember to celebrate! Someone today, somewhere was told otherwise. Go gal!" So this crazy adventure can be so easily summarized: it was a nothing that led to something that led to nothing.

Crap! I got caught up in the specialist who said it was nothing! I forgot there was still one more specialist to go. August 31st, 2011, I went to see the dermatologist. She took a look and thought it was Dermatitis Herpetiformis (DH), an allergic response to gluten. She took a skin biopsy from my knee to confirm. It pretty much means I have a rare form of Celiac, an autoimmune disease.

"Is it possible that is what was on my cervix?" I asked.

"Yes, type you have presents as herpes-like sores that break out on any skin surface." she told me, and then she said what so many others before her have said. "You are interesting; I haven't seen a case like yours in ages."

I half laughed. "It's not the first time I've heard that!" Yet somehow it appears all of this nonsense, seemingly cyclical, brought me back to where I started, and managed to reconnect me with purpose and reinforce my path to enlightenment along the way.

The End

*W*e went bowling on January 14th, 2012 and my mom was clearly depressed. When I broached the topic, she told me she was hoping she'd be dead by the end of the year. All I could say was "Wow." My crisis training told me I had to probe. It may have seemed insensitive, but the question needed to be asked. "That seems intense. Do you have any plans to assist the process?"

Her response was guilt inducing. She said "Don't call, and you won't find out."

As I considered how to best provide support without taking anything else on, my sister jumped in and made the decision for me. Emily told me "You have to tell her what you've been going through." Seriously, Emily, you needed to say that right in front of her? The circle of people aware of my medical issues was still quite small. I had to remind myself that Emily had good intentions. So, I told my mom about all the ultrasounds and the discussions about having a "likely benign growth." being on the verge of surgery, and about the fights with Eric and the recent multiple threats he has made to leave. Somehow my crap made her feel better.

I had a nasty dream last night, March 29, 2012. It started as a really fun party, seemingly with any guy who I've cared for, with lots of hugs, chats and friendly reunions. It then moved to a play date where I was getting too friendly with the dad (a completely unfamiliar person) and ended with full disclosure...Eric was packing...I said, "But I haven't had sex or kissed anyone!" I woke up and told him about the intense dream. It was a good conversation, but it still feels all too real. Do I say anything? Can I stay quiet? It was nothing, right? It was nothing.

March 30th. I was at home sick today, feeling like crap and trying to improve my state by lying in the hot tub. Instead of feeling better, I became hyper-alert and delusional. I closed my eyes and saw myself lying in a pool of blood. I opened my eyes and saw a man. I blinked and he was gone. I said "God help me! Heal my head!" In response I heard "My dear, you will always be crazy."

April 19th. Life sucks. I keep reflecting on that psychic I saw ages ago. She said I needed to walk alone to prove my strength. I'm back in that state I get into when my needs shift and every conversation seems meaningless and superficial. Perhaps it's not the need to walk alone so much as the need for someone to that fills my need for discussions about existence, purpose and paths. I feel so lost right now; there's been too much self-talk lately.

I'm so messed up. I feel like it's been way too long. It's May 15th, so it's been almost two months since that night I felt violated. That was a long overdue high (by the way, amazing). I wasn't prepared for the tears that followed (equally intense). I told him I was ok with him waking me up. It was just after I woke up, but I was no longer interested. I felt trapped, my sleepy mind sucked back into a time warp; there was no point in trying to say no again. He stopped, but my mind already spiralled. There was so much built-up hate when he didn't listen when I said stop. I hate my history. Either way, I managed to work myself high enough to conquer that hurdle. Now all I need to do is fix the way I feel when touched. Why are there so many triggers, so many memories, constant life challenges creeping up? I tell myself I am safe, but I don't believe it.

Today is June 18th. A good friend Mark, told me to focus on where I want to be: Eric is the father of my children. He helped me through my stuff in university, listened to my stories and stood by me when no one else would. I trusted him. He supported me after the kids were born and during my post-partum depression. I love him. I'm feeling kind of crazy for wanting more...but what? Eric has been through everything with me, so I should be able to support him and stand by him through whatever stress he is currently experiencing. I just feel so emotionally alone. I know love is a sacrifice. Kids will get older; there will be a shift in responsibility. A part of me needs that escape. I'm not in a spot where I'll take a risk. Kids are still young and need consistency, but I just want to run away for a weekend and take some time for myself. When will it be my turn to escape and think about me?

Isn't that what Ethan was saying?! Can we find new adventures? Maybe revisit the caves? Create a list of places to visit, things to accomplish? Yet the pull is so strong; is the fantasy the absence of kids? Maybe the issue is the absence of a five year plan. How can I think of where I want to be when what I want is an unknown adventure?

The songs are aligning in an obvious pattern this morning. Tears build. Why such extremes? There are highs to lows and I'm searching for my stabilizer. Someone once said I had to find happiness within before I could take care of anyone else. But the things that make me happy and those I derive pleasure from are often external. Is that because I am not happy or because I need regular reinforcement? I know I'm in a good spot. Is that sufficient to be happy? My standards for happiness have shifted. As I look out into the herd of people riding the subway, thoughts of my life are reinforced. I am in a good spot, but then why do I feel such intense emotion?

June 28th. He lost his temper again. We talked about the last outburst near Emily's birthday. My response was extreme. I feel like my world is falling apart. He's been threatening to leave for months now.

"I don't care what you do. The kids don't listen." he said.

"I don't know how to help." I responded.

"Maybe I'll just drink more, like you do." he said.

Ouch. Perhaps I am drinking too much. Perhaps I'm over-searching for an escape. Perhaps I just don't want to continue with the crap before me. I feel alone, Mark is the only one who seems good at grounding me lately, talking me in circles and grounding me with my basic wants and beliefs. He somehow asks questions that seem random, which dig inside my mind and I end up answering the next question with "I love Eric." Or "I love my boys." He reminds me of the importance that everyone is healthy. We are doing ok financially. Many people would be envious of what I have. I need to focus on the positive; there is so much in my life that is good. I need to believe we can get back to a good spot. Mark is good at giving me the kick in the ass I need. Eric's loss of temper is so mild compared to any memory I have of my dad. I know I'm over-sensitive to any form of anger. That's my issue.

Eric has been so good since the outburst. It's been three days, and while he is clearly pissed and not talking to me, he's been a really good dad. I remember loving the days after the abuse… I can't help but see patterns from my own childhood. I recognize a spark of rage in his eyes, and that brings me back to my abuse. He is not my father. He is a good dad. It's just that I'm feeling sick, medicated, and my mind is taking it too far, that look triggered memories that scared me. Clearly my past still haunts me.

I was sick and stayed home Friday, mostly from illness, partly from fear. It's just been messed up. We had a long discussion yesterday about needing to talk while we still can. I started looking at condos in the neighbourhood. We could live in the same building on different floors. It could be an easy transition. He is so stressed out lately, and he's still threatening to leave, so maybe it's time.

We had talked about taking a trip. Maybe that's all it was, talk. As the time approached, the trip became a local thing, and he decided he'd work. I decided I'd take the kids on my own. I planned a slow driving trip through some scenic areas nearby. We'd go at the kids' speed and find hotels along the way.

There were so many highs and lows this past year. 2012 was crazy. If ever given the choice, I would never choose to repeat it. Evan needed a circumcision, Ethan needed to get his tonsils and adenoids out, and it seemed like I needed to jump on the surgery band wagon.

Saturday, August 18th, we had Katya come over to babysit. I was cashing in on my birthday present from her, a 24 hour coupon for babysitting. Eric and I were heading out for dinner with his friend Daren from university and his wife Melinda. I was leaving with the boys on Monday. Daren and Melinda put a lot of effort into making a gluten-free dinner to meet my dietary restrictions. The food was good and we went onto the patio for drinks before dessert. We were coming in from the patio and I felt nauseous. I went white, and then start sweating despite feeling freezing. I went upstairs to the washroom. Had I had too much to drink? I had a cider before dinner and a glass of wine with dinner. I didn't feel drunk, but I felt I was stepping out of my body as the world shimmered as if all was a mirage. Suddenly, the urge to vomit overcame me. Up came dinner, and then lunch, and then breakfast.

I felt exhausted and pain was flooding over me. I went to lie down in their spare bedroom. The pain got steadily more intense. I touched my stomach to find the small umbilical hernia I had when pregnant with Evan was humongous! While throwing up, it appeared my intestines had burst through. My hernia was huge. It was very hot to touch and extremely painful!

"I think I have to go to the hospital." I said. As they tried to find out which hospital was closest, the pain continued to grow exponentially. We started to drive, not knowing the destination; Google maps could not pinpoint the nearest emergency room on any of our phones. I knew local hospitals. I told them the name of one I knew to be close by, but it was taking too long.

"I can't continue." I said. The pain was too intense, they called 911. When the ambulance showed up, my memories started to blur. I remember asking the woman in the back of the ambulance how much longer it would be until we got to the hospital.

"Seven minutes." she said.

I must have asked again "Five minutes." she told me.

The pain didn't let up. "Almost there." she said trying to be supportive. I remember moaning in pain, it was so intense.

We were finally at the hospital, but there was no reprieve. The emergency room was very busy; there were multiple traumas, so I was a lower priority. It was clearly a crazy night. After I threw up again, my hernia bulged further and a nurse gave me some morphine. The x-ray showed the intestines were blocked and the CT scan showed they were pinched and needed to surgically be reinserted. By morning, two of the people above me in triage succumbed to their injuries. I finally made it into the queue, hoping I wouldn't be the next to succumb.

They moved me up to the sixth floor to await surgery, but it was 1:45pm and my morphine was wearing out. I was told that the two hour intervals had gone to six hours and I could not be given more morphine. Finally, when I was in a semi-private room with a bed instead of on the stretcher in the makeshift space they had allotted me in the hallway of the ER. It was Sunday and Eric went to get his first snack in 18 hours. In his absence, the pain steadily increased until I couldn't handle it and screamed tears of pain for what seemed like an eternity. Eric returned. A nurse came to see what was going on and found someone to overrule what could only be a transcribing error. It was three in the afternoon before I got more medication.

I was called at four in the afternoon to go for surgery. We hung out in a hallway for about an hour as my pain medication started wearing off again. I agreed to the epidural and tuned out for the rest of the pre-surgery info after they said "and possibility of death." I simply signed when and where they asked me to. The doctor talked about cutting out a section of my intestines, a blood transfusion, and on and on and on...

They then took me into a room, gave me the epidural and some oxygen, and I started counting backwards from 10. After surgery, the recovery room was a bit intense. I'm not sure if Shawn (the guy next to me) was handcuffed to his bed, but he kept making rattling sounds and was swearing in every sentence. Shawn was a very angry guy, complaining about everything: not having eaten all day, not getting to see his girlfriend that often and how long we were waiting for patient transfer! The nurses were close to calling security a few times and were clear in explaining that to him when he made threats. He asked what security would do, and when he learned that they would just keep him in the bed, he seemed to change his behaviour. I guess he was hoping security would take him out of recovery. The surgeon was ok with my recovery and he gave me clearance to leave.

My blood pressure was low; hanging out at 90, so the floor refused me. Stuck for another half hour, I used breathing techniques and movements to raise my blood pressure. I have an irregular regular heart beat, so my heart speeds up when I inhale and slows down as I exhale. The nurse also assisted by topping me up with a bag of fluid and I made it to 110! That was four points higher than pre-operation. Security then showed up. I thought the nurses finally called about Shawn; however they were looking for me. Evidently Eric and mom were told I'd be up in about 30 minutes, and that had been two hours ago! They wanted to know I was still alive. The post-operative floor nurses never told them that they refused to admit me to the floor, and then patient transfer took forever! It was 10:30 before I finally got up to my room and saw my mom and Eric.

It looked like I was recovering well; they discharged me on day three, after my digestive system appeared to be working. At home I had a great sleep, and I managed to eat some solid food. It stayed down for a few hours before it all came up again. After throwing up for the fifth time, it was obvious the content was intestinal. Mom took me back to the emergency room. They put me on morphine and IV drip. After a few hours, they told me it was just dehydration and discharged me. I was home for less than three hours before she drove me back again, as the intestinal vomiting continued. This time they did a CT scan and discovered my intestines were blocked, perhaps swollen shut and they admitted me again. They tried to give me a nasogastric intubation (NG tube) in through my nose to empty the rest of my stomach contents, to ease the pressure on my intestines. The nurse in ER attempted unsuccessfully, and when I started gagging and coughing in pain she ripped the tube out, traumatizing my nose. I held gauze to it as it bled for over 20 minutes. She told me they'd have to try again once I was transferred to the unit.

Terrified, nauseous, in pain and exhausted they transferred me upstairs. I was told the nurse was going to try the NG tube again. I asked for some morphine first. They gave me water to sip as they did the insert unsuccessfully a second time. At least this nurse poked around slowly and when she accepted it would be unsuccessful she removed it slowly. In tears of pain, exhaustion and frustration I said I was done and they agreed to let me sleep. The surgeon was going to have to try again later. After my nap, he came to give me the NG tube. They decided they were going to try the smallest adult tube they had. Again I asked for morphine, so he came back in 20 minutes allowing time for it to kick in. I knew the pain to come and the blood that would follow. I hoped the skill level of the surgeon would be better. The resident attempted first on my left nostril, and after determining my nasal path was not passable, the surgeon tried my right, also unsuccessful.

"Interesting." he said, "You must be one of the rare people that it won't work on." I'm so sick of being interesting! "Did you have any nose surgery?"

"No." I said in pain, sounding nasal although gauze was plugging my nose.

"I guess we will just have to wait and see." They dismissed it, as though it just wouldn't work. Really, that was all they could say after six bloody attempts?

Eric came to visit again with the boys. Evan still seemed scared. Ethan was chatty, it was a welcomed distraction. Later Mom came to visit as well. Emily's foot rubs were great at calming me as well. Days started to merge. Mom and Emily helped out by watching the kids so Eric could come and visit on his own. Eric snuggled in my hospital bed and we watched a movie.

I'm back to vomiting. My third CT scan is booked for 10:30 this morning. The doctor said "Just so you are fully informed: you may need a second surgery. I will try to do that this afternoon around four." I've reached my ultimate low. I just want to feel healthy again, but the path back seems to have so many obstacles. I have no fight left in me.

How do I get my head back in the game? How can I think of where I want to be and get there? What happened to the positive energy of yesterday? It was so optimistic; so promising. Purpose, reasoning, growth: I had understanding yesterday. It is better! Make me believe that! I feel like just running away and living on juice, liquid meals slowly draining through my destroyed intestines. Solid food had smacked me down the day before. The pain was so intense. Morphine felt like defeat. Exhaustion and fatigue covered me like a blanket, fever and chills alternately sucking me down deeper into an abyss.

"I form my consequences!" I yell into nothingness. I can think myself out of this crap, right? I pick myself up, walk to the hallway window, return to bed and collapse.

"Defeated? Is that possible?" I cry into my pillow.

I'm in a serious funk. I'm so tired of trying to be optimistic, so tired of being sick. I'm tired of the tears, tired of the pain, tired of the guilt, tired of being tired, of feeling I can't do this anymore. It is August 30th, and this has been going on now for 12 days. I have nothing left to give. My stomach and head hurt from crying. I no longer see a path home...I'm not getting better.

I've been on fluids for two weeks; they decided I needed a Total Parenteral Nutrition (TPN) line. It is a way to feed me intravenously without me having to eat or digest. Normally, it goes in a pic line (a large vein close to the heart) but because the specialized technicians had left for the weekend, it was going in my hand. It was less than two hours before it was painful, and at six hours I could no longer sleep, even with the morphine drip. The pain was a constant irritating level five out of ten. It was all I could do to distract myself by pacing the halls like a zombie, exhausted and in tears.

Joe tried to keep up my spirits all night by texting while everyone on this side of the country slept. His mom was also in the hospital. I had an image of her being at the same hospital as me. I was connected to my IV pole and sitting at her bedside. "I love your son." I told her and sat listening as she told me stories about Joe. I fell in to a quick dream state. It was the only sleep I had all night. At morning rounds, I begged the resident to take the line out. I had kept down two fruit drinks with added protein, and promised to have another. When it was removed, relief from pain was not immediate, as it still took time to clear my veins of the fat and protein solution they had been pumping into my small vein.

I had enough; on September 2nd I asked to be released. There was nothing more they could do for me. The NG tube didn't work, the TPN line didn't work, and the only thing they could do was give me morphine and fluids. I wanted to be home. I was feeling hopeless, but at least they let me go. I was finally home. I went upstairs when things got intense; lying in bed in intense pain, I began praying. But I couldn't hear God; I couldn't feel the presence and I couldn't see the light. I was stuck in a deep fog. Trying to get up through the fog, in tears I continued praying.

The response was "You don't deserve to heal, you are not pure. You can't heal until you've purged." It wasn't only my stomach contents; it was my sins as well. It was time. I was in tears and I needed a full purge, this time of my mind, not stomach. I sent Eric a text asking him to come home.

In a tearful moment of self-blame I told Eric I had brought all of this on myself. I told him I had gotten too close to a friend at work a few months ago and things went further than they should have. I needed to preface, we didn't have sex, I didn't kiss him, but things went emotionally and physically too far. He was disappointed. I messed up. I can't predict what will change. He said he wasn't planning to leave, and apologized that threatening to leave had made me feel alone and unloved. We talked, and he has improved so much. Evan and Ethan seem to have grown up these last few weeks. I had tried speaking with a social worker and chaplain while in hospital, but it wasn't them I needed to be talking to. It's like everyone else got better except me.

September 25th. I was put on anti-depressants. I prefer to know how I feel than have it masked. I'm only going to try it for 20 days to see if it affects the vomiting, then wean off them. I needed to develop a plan to get off them before I even started. I talked to Eric about my concerns, and needed to know about the drug and how it responds. I haven't been talking to John, Joe, Katya or anyone from work. I seem to have successfully alienated myself from those closest to me. Eric, on the other hand has been amazing, with the kids, the house and me. He stays with me when I vomit, rinses my bowl, rubs my back, holds my hair; he has shown endless love.

I finally made it back to work; I've been told symptoms will continue to persist. It's a struggle, but all of that drama actually pulled my family back together. I had a coffee with Debra, a friend from work, and she asked "So, what choice do you think you made this time?" Telling Eric what had happened had been the safe decision. Choosing to work on this relationship, choosing to try therapy, choosing to help the kids get over this, choosing to stay… it was all the best choices. But I wonder if the relationship is salvageable. So much has happened. So much has been said, so much damage caused. Eric still has yet to get angry at me for the confession in September. He keeps saying we will deal with it when I get healthy.

March 21, 2013. I feel like I'm going to die. My stomach is whirling in pain. I'm wishing it would end. I can't seem to induce vomiting, so all I've been doing is adjusting my position with each stabbing contraction and dealing with it until it subsides. My liquid morphine is no longer helping. I can't go back to the hospital. I fear I won't come out. Wow! That last one was ridiculous. I pray to God, give this purpose or take it away.

Ethan (now eight), seemingly in tune with me, is sleepwalking. I try to be quiet. I hear him talking in a rhythmic pattern, words incoherent to me down the hall in my bedroom. But he returns to his room and is seemingly back to sleep. Then suddenly the urge for release; I go to my ensuite and the pain erupts and is purged into to toilet. It was only stomach contents, though, so I know it's going to be a long night. Did he know? Were his words purposeful in inducing my vomit? He has powers and abilities beyond my skill set. I washed my mouth and face and returned to bed. Moments later, I knew it wouldn't work. I got back up and had a shower to try and reduce the cramping. The heat, as warm as I can tolerate, turned my skin a rosy pink.

The stabbing pain and contractions ease, so I stand there a while longer focused only on my breathing and Reiki, letting universal energy fill me with each breath and the hot water wash away the pain. Successful at inducing a comfy, sleepy state, I dried off, put on warm pyjamas and crawled back into bed.

Alright God, what's the purpose? What's the message I'm suppose to get? And then he appears. "She's ready."

I don't feel afraid, as I had before. I think he's right, that I am ready. I say to Eric, "I think I'm going to die."

"Why?" he asked, with clear concern.

"Because he said I was ready." I said.

"Who said?" Eric snuggled up, cuddling me.

"I don't know his name." I respond.

"I'm Scott." I hear him say.

"He said his name is Scott." I relay.

"I want you to stay." Eric says, getting emotional and holding me tight. Scott disappeared and I fell asleep in Eric's arms.

The stomach pain continues in intense waves of excruciating pain, awakening me. I continue to purge each time the biggest waves crest. I no longer think this is food-related. There are moments I can't breathe, my body seizing with the intense stabbing pain. Slapping the bed, Eric comes to my side. It was over 40 seconds that time. My intestines, stomach and esophagus all seized together to purge intestinal content, preventing me from taking a breath. Finally I gasped for air, wondering if next time may be my last. The last time I looked at the clock was 2:17am. I'm so exhausted I don't know how much longer I can continue.

How do I say goodbye? I have a flash of a written letter to each person dear to me and key information all on my computer in a file called "you know the password." with letters to my sons. Edits to my autobiography are in my work bag...I have an email with the contact and package info for a self-publishing company. There are a few last things I need to do. My mind drifts into planning and falls asleep.

My alarm went off at 4:55am. I feel like crap, but go through the motions of getting ready for work. Everything but my pyjamas was too tight on my belly. I settled on a long sleeve cotton t-shirt with a big comfy-yet-professional sweater. I'm thankful I have a student and my day won't be too hard. I look in the fridge, wondering what I may want to eat for lunch. Nausea instantly floods me. I pack two pieces of gluten-free bread and a banana. I got my shoes on and pondered taking the car or transit. Nausea turned to intense cramping, and I didn't think I could walk to the subway, but my car was low on gas. I take off my shoes and go to the washroom, but it was only dry heaving. I make it back to the sofa, not sure I can make it out of the house. I close my eyes and take five minutes to calm my body.

I called in sick and crawled back into my bed. I woke up to Evan lying beside me; he carefully got out on the other side of the bed. The blanket was pulled up over my head, but he must have seen me. He walked around to my side of the bed and said "Mom?"

"Um." was all I could muster in response, my throat feeling sore from all the vomiting.

"Remember you said you were going to pick me up early today so we can watch a movie?" he said.

"Yes, Evan." I responded and he scampered off to get dressed and went down stairs. The weird thing was that I used to hide when I was home sick. If he saw me, his whole morning would be messed up, and drop off would be hard, since he'd want to stay home. But now having turned five almost three months ago, he seems to be growing up so much.

So here I lay. Physically exhausted, face shoved in my pillow, one eye open writing what may be some of my last words. The house is now so quiet. Maybe I'll just take one more nap, before I finish. But I do have to reflect: if today was my last day, what would I want to do?

March 27. Death lingers near me, reminding me I haven't yet written my goodbye letters. "I'm still here," he said "you can't run away."

I shake my head. "How much longer do I have? Do I see myself at Ethan's birthday? Will I make it to the summer vacation I've planned to the west coast and stampede?" I ask.

"Write the letters!" I hear. Is that my higher self doing the talking, or death? I'm currently feeling paranoid. It's hard to know when to ride out the burst of anxiety and when to crush it with medication. I often ask God what the purpose of this moment is. As I try to identify the source of anxiety, I realize it is in the saying goodbye. I know everyone will be fine without me and I feel I've left enough good memories to be remembered. But to say goodbye, is hard. Whom do I write to first? The easy ones? The hard ones? How do I say goodbye? What would I want my final email or text to say? What do I want Eric to send out to those who made a difference in my life?

If it had to be a text would I make it all encompassing? "I feel like death is upon me and I need to prepare for goodbyes. The last year has been a crazy rollercoaster of ridiculous highs and lows in all aspects of life. Thank you for the moments we shared and the memories you have given me. I treasured the good moments, enjoyed life, and cherished the challenges for the change and growth."

But so many people had key impacts and there are relationships I love and cherish. That's not enough. I need to say more. But what can I say to them? "I treasured our talks. Thank you for being a part of my life." That's too generic. The ones who mean a lot to me could read into it, but those in my life who think they matter would also feel like they were included. That was harsh. People who think they matter. The most I could say to everyone is: "Think of that moment you felt like we connected, that deep conversation, the words that escaped your lips unfiltered. Those are the moments I loved! I loved being trusted with your secrets and your life challenges. It didn't matter where we were or what we were doing, it was the one-on-one discussion that made me feel valued and important in your life, which in turn made you important in mine." Nothing feels like it is sufficient or all-encompassing.

Eric: *Wow. It sucks to feel like this is goodbye. The last few years have been so intense. I truly am sorry for putting you through so much crap. I'm not sure there is anything I can say right now that would be helpful. I do love you. My life was better with you in it. We had so many good times. We got together in 1997. If I could wipe away all the drama from the last two years this letter would be much better. You were there for all of it, through the stories of my trauma in our early days, the therapy, the emotional growth. You gave me everything I wanted. It was because of you that my spectrum of happiness grew and I wanted more because I learned that obtaining happiness was possible. I lay in bed and told you that I thought I was going to die and you held on to me and said you are not ready for me to go. I believe you are the only reason I am still here and able to write my final goodbyes.*

Your love has provided me with so much strength over the last 15 years. The struggles we face are nothing compared to what we have overcome. Thank you for all you have given me. When I think of what you did that made me love you most, it was the little things. I never felt more loved than when you cared for me. It was at my lowest moments when you held my hair, rubbed my back and washed out the basin that made me feel you would be there for me though anything. It was that love that I feel pulled us back together and washed away the challenges of the last two years.

I love you. I've always loved you. From our walk early on with the lunch box guys and the storm, to you protecting me from the falling branches, you were always there to protect me from the big and the little. Your supportive presence that day in the library provided the opportunity for so much healing. I treasured your supportive arms during labour, the endless support during renovations and work on the house as we merged it with my dreams. I appreciated the prompt responses to my immediate needs, be they phone calls stating I've had enough, telling you the baby is in his crib crying and I'm going to have a shower, the numerous times I've requested you come home right then, and you left work to take care of us. I know I complained work was a priority, but when we really needed you, you always came. I love you.

Ethan: As much as I wish I had the perfect words to say to you, it seems they are impossible to find. I loved you so much! One of my favourite recent moments was when you and Evan decided to make each other dinner; you worked together, yet independently you chose what you thought the other would want. Both of you were bringing out a bowl for the other to munch in front of the TV. When I commented, Evan said, "We were making stuff for each other because we are best brothers." After this, Evan gave you a big hug and you returned it. I wish for you to feel loved and to love freely. Sometimes you seem to hold on to your anger and hate. I hope you can let that go and focus on the good moments.

I loved watching you grow up. Your humour was always a source of laughter. We could never predict the things that came out of your mouth! As a baby, you had such a big belly laugh for simple things, like a bag swept up into the air and then allowed to slowly fall to the floor on its own. Your humour refined, as most children's does, and you came up with nonsense knock-knock jokes, but by the age of three you started to form creative out-of-the-box thoughts and processes. You came up with a brilliant ASL joke: "Bored, you?" as a perfect question, but without words it appears you are picking your nose and offering what you found. At age five, you understood currency and offered your babysitter $2 to see her breasts. When she turned that down, you increased the amount to $200! I've written many stories that illustrated how you were a quick thinker and gave lots of immediate responses that always seemed so clever.

Your adventurous nature always led us to explore new places. You challenged me to find new parks, new playgrounds, and new indoor play areas. Your love for nature was often masked by your disdain for repetition. I still remember your excitement one morning when you came into the kitchen repeating "Pink and blue! Pink and blue!" You were two years old and thrilled to see the beautiful sunrise. It was you who led us to different farms, pick-your-own orchards and maple festivals. You also seemed to connect with nature in a way few others do. From a young age, you seemed to communicate with animals. At the aquarium the dolphins listened to you when you signed for them to "come play" and stopped when you signed "finished." Emily got it all on video. You seemed to connect with dogs and cats in the park, or random animals in the neighbourhood. They would seem to come to you and you seemed receptive to it. You also seemed to crave adventure and loved thrill rides. As early as I can remember, you loved the early rides at small amusement parks and as you got older, larger theme parks became the new thrill source.

As you continue to grow, I want you to use your strengths, but also work on your weaknesses. You have such a capacity to love, and I fear you put up walls to protect yourself and won't let others in. We all need love. I hope you will find friends in your life that you can love, trust and share all your stories with. With you, it was always hard to tell when you wanted people around and when you wanted quiet. You often wanted big parties, but mid-party would disappear for some quiet time. Please remember to mix it up with social experiences. Have some big parties and create some amazing memories, as well as find the quality in small group interactions to form lasting bonds of friendship.

I loved you so much from the first moment I saw you, a love so deep beyond any love I experienced before. You were mine, a tiny precious bundle, dependent on me to love and nurture. As I watched you grow, I knew I needed to step back and let you make your own mistakes and learn from them. I loved that sometimes the lessons were obvious. Like the time you wanted to play on the Xbox instead of study for your math test. You said you knew your stuff and I said it was your choice. When your results came back poorly, you said maybe next time you should study, and the next test results were great! I know very few of life's lessons will be that obvious, but with your intuition, I believe that upon reflection, you will find purpose to all of your challenges and lessons that will help shape you into the person you want to become! Never stop dreaming!

Evan: My boy, you never ceased to amaze me. You were the most huggy, snuggly person I had ever known, so full of love! I hope that always continues for you. You could never seem to get enough hugs and snuggles. I wore you for the first few months of your life. I often woke up with you snuggled up beside me. You always had such big hugs, in the morning, after school, at bed time and sometimes just because. In the first few years of your life, I have hugged and been hugged by you more than anyone else in my entire life! I loved you so much!

You had so much power and control over your body too. You were walking before ten months, climbing on to the kitchen counters using the knobs on the drawers by 12 months, playing ball and Frisbee by 18 months and continually excelling and surprising us with every sport or kinetic skill you attempted. You could do somersaults really early on, and we went to gymnastics you could climb the rope at just after you turned four! You did cartwheels through the living room and had a fascination with dancing and moving your body any way you could discover.

You were always big for your age, and even the doctor didn't believe your height. You were almost 3'6" when we went for your two year check-up. The doctor insisted you were three years old until she confirmed your birth year in your chart. She said you were going to be close to seven feet tall!

I loved watching you grow and develop. I could never predict what you would do next; your interests kept changing. You were always into sports and video games, but you would go through phases of activity preferences. At two, you loved painting. You would mix paints and make deliberate shapes, patterns and colourful marks on paper in very artistic ways. You would go through paints and canvases so quickly that it was always hard to choose favourites to keep, hang up or put in your art book. At three, however, it seemed like you had no currency. All you wanted was me. You would ask me questions like why I married daddy and tell me I should have married you. The only punishment I could offer that would bother you was to put me in time out, and say that you couldn't sit or snuggle or play with me until you showed us you could be gentle. You had so much power and strength that it was hard for you to figure out how to be gentle during play. At four, you started to develop some interests in material possessions: you loved hot wheel cars, remote control cars, sticker books, gems and presents. It seemed like you could never get enough. Even with over 150 cars, you still saw more you wanted. Your sticker books almost seemed like a status symbol in school and day care. You had buddies who would help you finish the entire book within a day or two. Then, at five you did a quick shift into writing and drawing. You had over five journals you made notes and drawings in. If you didn't bring the current one to school, you would make one there using post-it notes and stapling them together to make a book. You also became interested in cooking, sitting on the counter, or standing on a chair to make dinner. "I'm the chef tonight!" you would say, and come up with elaborate dinner menus.

Many times I looked at you falling asleep in my arms and wondered what you would be like in ten years. You had so much energy, so many loves and so much potential. I hoped you would be able to tame your temper, and as you started forming solid friendships there was a steady improvement. I remember reflecting on how you often feel loved through physical proximity and material possessions, and how you would often ask us to buy small tokens to give to your friends, showing them love in the way you felt and understood it best.

I'm never sure how much you'll remember, but if my friend Scott was as important to me in kindergarten to leave such a lasting impression, I believe you will always remember Rachel. I hope you develop good friendships with children who encourage you to behave and excel. I can't imagine not getting to see you grow up, but just in case I don't make it, I need you to slow yourself down sometimes and snuggle with daddy, hang out with your close friends and remember to build good bonds with people. You were always so active and busy, and it is important to take some quiet time to balance that lifestyle. I have no doubt you will find love. You seem to let people in so quickly and love so freely, and I need to know you will be good to your brother too. You guys will need each other as you get older. There will be many disagreements, but I believe you can face your challenges together and come up with better ideas through teamwork! You have so much power in the way you love, so hold on to that and you will amaze yourself! I believe in you!

There are others I would want to say goodbye to, the people who have made a major impact in my life. Emily and my Mom are the only family I consider family. There were only a small group of those I loved and trusted with my stories as they happened; Joe, Katya, Mark, Martyn, Christina, and Carmela… It is such a small group, to whom I've exposed my vulnerabilities, and all of them had essential roles in my life; all of them individually know how much I valued our interactions and the impact our relationship had on my life.

So there it was. I wrote the letters, after surviving 12 crazy intense months I'd never choose to repeat. I took some time to reflect. I drifted off to sleep and had another dream. I couldn't tell if God was dying, asking

for help, or trying to get me to take him more fully into myself. I titled it
God is in me.

I was at the riverside watching the traffic and playing with
my boys. God appeared to me as a voice, and then as an old man
at my side.

"It's time." he said. "I need your help."

The rock in the water shimmered as if calling to me, so I
picked it up. The bridge in the distance started to collapse. "Help."
he said to me.

I squeezed the rock. The bridge froze. The cars that were on
it as it started to shake stopped too, and then almost as if I willed
them, they unfroze and drove safely off the bridge. I released
the rock and the bridge collapsed a bit more. Holding the rock,
God at my side, I thought healing thoughts and the bridge slowly
repaired, lifting, repairing and returning to functionality.

Continuing on our way, God continued to walk beside me.
Teaching me, he spoke: "The rock was only a tangible item. The
power is in you. I am in you."

Next, the waves were rushing and a boat was in peril. I
clenched my fists without the rock. Thinking healing thoughts, I
heard God's voice. "Calm the waters; heal the world." The waves
calmed and the boat and its passengers were safe.

The next scene flashed before me. Evan, Ethan, God and
I were climbing a dark metal staircase, seemingly high outside
a building; we could see the dark storm clouds rolling in. The
horizon was fraught with turmoil. "Clear the sky." He told me.

This time with a hand wave, I pushed the darkness away and
it dissolved, leaving the blue sky and bright sun shining down
on us. As if in a flash we are inside a mall, and someone on the
mezzanine was looking over in despair. I had a premonition of
her jumping.

"Help her." God tells me. I envisioned God's arms around her in a hug, easing the pain, offering hope. My arms were an extension of his, and he consumed me. "I am in you."

When I awoke, the peace was overwhelming. The Reiki running through me felt so strong. Everything had an energy shimmer this morning. Still the feeling that everything is over persists. I tied to dismiss the crazy, but it continues to nudge at me. It's time to say goodbye. I hear the voice calling to me. The trees are waving, the water flowing, and my gaze is captured as nature bids me adieu. Peace consumes me. I close my eyes. The warmth of the sun on my skin, the brightness shining through my closed eyes reminds me of the vast beauty I'm ignoring. Life. Death. Meaning. Purpose. Goals.

I feel ready to move on, yet terrified about my six month follow-up tests. The vomiting has continued well after surgery. The doctor did say that if I wasn't one hundred percent gluten free, she won't be looking for cancer, she will have found it. Will I have cancer? Is it something worse? Why am I still throwing up so long after the surgery?

I was sitting in the medical office, when an elderly woman came in with a cane. I got up to offer her my seat next to the door. Did I choose it so I could run away?

She told me "You are kind." as I held her hand to assist her balance as she moved to sit while her husband waited in line for her.

I say, "You have to be kind as you await tests that terrify you."

"You are too young to be sick." she told me.

"I didn't know age was a factor with disease. I see so many babies in special care nurseries." I said.

"I'm 87 and have been through a lot, but medicine has made such advances." she continued.

"Hmm, I didn't know you could run away from death. If it's my time, medical advances won't help." I told her.

"Angela?" Whether or not it was a coincidence or timing, I stood up. The woman behind the counter looked at me and announced, "It's your turn."

Acknowledgements

Life is one endless journey. My great thanks go to my husband Eric who has been incredibly supportive to me during my life, illness and writing process.

My family was an integral part of my success. Lana, my mom encouraged me to dream and write, Emily was always there on whatever platform I needed her, and my boys, Ethan and Evan, who filled my life with love, laughter and curiosity. I would also like to thank John and Hilda for sharing the family history stories.

Thank you to Nicholas and Claire who were the first to thoroughly read my autobiography and provide feedback and to Katie and Adam for their time to take photos of my token memories, and to iUniverse for all their knowledge and suggestions to refine my work.

Finally I need to give a big thank you to all of my friends and co-workers who supported me along my journey out of darkness and listened to me tell my stories along my autobiographical process.

Thank you!